The Belles Heures

OF

Jean, Duke of Berry

The Belles Heures

OF

Jean, Duke of Berry

THE CLOISTERS

THE METROPOLITAN MUSEUM OF ART

MILLARD MEISS

AND

ELIZABETH H. BEATSON

GEORGE BRAZILLER   NEW YORK

The original manuscript of *The Belles Heures* of the
Duke of Berry is in The Cloisters Collection of the
Metropolitan Museum of Art. The manuscript was
purchased for The Cloisters Collection in 1954 with
funds provided by John D. Rockefeller, Jr.

Published in 1974
All rights reserved. No part of the contents of this book
may be reproduced without the written consent of the publisher,
George Braziller, Inc.
One Park Avenue, New York, N.Y. 10016

Library of Congress Catalog Card Number 74-75688
Printed in France by Draeger, Paris
Bound in Switzerland by Mayer and Soutter

Miniatures photographed by Charles Passela
Book Design by Vincent Torre
Slipcase and Binding Design by Oscar Ratti

To John Plummer

First Author in this Series and Generous Adviser

Contents

INTRODUCTION

BY MILLARD MEISS

The *Belles Heures* of the Duke of Berry, in private possession until 1954, is much less well known than the *Très Riches Heures*. Painted by the three Limbourg Brothers just before they turned to the *Très Riches Heures*, it contains superlative qualities no longer visible in its famous successor. For the Limbourgs as for Monet, passing from his *Gare Saint-Lazare* to his haystacks, growth and change entailed sacrifices.

The *Belles Heures* and the *Très Riches Heures*, painted just a few years apart, differ so much from each other because of the combination of exceptional artists with an exceptional patron. The Duke of Berry created for the youthful illuminators a remarkably stimulating environment. They were surrounded by a great collection and by learned men who proposed ideas for novel themes and for new ways of representing old themes In this atmosphere the artists, or at least Paul, the greatest among the brothers, evolved a new sense of the value of originality. To the delight of his patron he persevered in the search for individual patterns of form and unseen aspects of the natural world.

That the Duke of Berry was pleased with the progress of the *Belles Heures* we cannot doubt. Only a show of interest by him and his circle would have encouraged the brothers to contemplate so many changes—changes which, as we shall see, they must have felt they had the time to execute. At an early stage the Duke apparently gave the painters the sense of a secure livelihood, so that, freed of the necessity to seek commissions elsewhere, they could concentrate on the quality of their work for him. Shortly after the completion of the *Belles Heures* he asked them to undertake a second prayer book, soon described as the *Très Riches Heures*. These were surely the best commissions illuminators anywhere in Europe at this time could win.

Life had shouldered the Duke of Berry with many obligations, but it also offered him great possibilities. As the son, brother, and uncle of three successive kings of France and the ruling duke of the south central part of the realm he had the usual options of great princes. He naturally played a role, at times important, in affairs of state, but he early proved to care much less about political power and warfare than his brothers or nephews. His manuscripts contain few political allusions. If there is one in the representation of a Burgundian chateau in the *Itinerary* (223v) it probably concerns an attempt to mediate between the two opposing French factions. The portrait of the Duke presents him in prayer (91), and indeed in the initial version of it his ducal coronet was apparently not included—he wore only a turban. His enthusiasm for the unusual subject of Aracoeli (26v) derived partly from a wish to associate himself with the Emperor Augustus, but Augustus as a cultivated ruler of the Roman Empire at the moment when he has a vision of the infant Christ.

In a family distinguished for its interest in works of art—the beautiful prayerbook of Jean de Berry's mother is now not inappropriately preserved in the Cloisters alongside the *Belles Heures*[1]—the Duke became the greatest collector of all. As the pace of his acquisitions increased, by commission, purchase, and gift, he decided to keep records, and from 1402 on these inventories approach in their accuracy, fullness, and chronological order the work of a modern museum registrar. It is these unprecedented records that disclose to us the enormous range of the collection, for all the objects have vanished except the tapestries in the Cloisters, a sparkling enameled gold reliquary in the British Museum, several beautiful ancient and pseudo-antique cameos in the Louvre, and copies of the related gold medals of the Roman emperors, famous in their time and in Renaissance Italy.

These medals and other objects in the collection fascinated the Duke's illuminators. In the *Belles Heures*, for instance, the scene of the Emperor Heraclius at the gate of Jerusalem (156) is closely connected with the medal of Heraclius. The ancient and medieval objects assembled by the Duke from near and far, from Italy and Byzantium as well as from northern Europe, enriched the experience of his artists much as comparable later collections were to do—the collections of the Medici or the popes and, eventually, the public museum. Indeed the sculptures, golden reliefs, crosses, reliquaries, and manuscripts that Jean de Berry gave to the Sainte-Chapelle at Bourges made this building serve not only as his mortuary chapel but a museum of contemporary religious art.

Curiously, it is not only the works in precious materials or the panels and the tapestries that have almost entirely disappeared but also the stoutest of the Duke's possessions—his buildings. What has come down to us in unique number is his group of objects with the least intrinsic value and little practical use; we have about 100 of his 300 illuminated manuscripts. Although manuscripts represented one of the less costly parts of the collection, not nearly as expensive as rubies and gold plate, there is evidence to show that the Duke held them in special esteem. To the more highly prized of them he added jeweled covers and bookmarks. He regularly wrote his ex-libris in all of them in his beautiful hand, and occasionally, as in the *Belles Heures*, he asked his scribe Jean Flamel to proclaim his ownership in a display of rhapsodic script (1). Another clear sign of the Duke's love of his illuminated books is his attitude toward his illuminators. In an age when the identities of craftsmen were seldom disclosed by signatures, and when almost all the makers of objects in the vast ducal collection remained nameless in the inventories, four artists are recorded as the authors of illuminated manuscripts. All these manuscripts have survived, and one of them, the *Très Riches Heures*, was manifestly painted by the same masters who executed the *Belles Heures*.

We know from a series of documents unequaled in their time that these brothers, Paul, Jean, and Herman, were the sons of a sculptor of Nijmegen (now Holland) and the nephews of Jean Malouel, the painter of the Duke of Burgundy, who had earlier come to Paris and Dijon from the same northern town. Two of them, Jean and Herman, described as "jonnes enfans," were apprenticed in 1399 to a goldsmith in Paris. From 1402 to 1404 Paul and Jean were paid for painting miniatures in a *Bible moralisée*. In our opinion this Bible, often said to be lost, exists in the Bibliothèque nationale in Paris, the earliest known work of the boys.[2] They received the commission for it from the Duke of Burgundy, Philippe le Hardi, whose enthusiasm for illumination had been kindled by his brother and close friend, Jean de Berry. The two Limbourg boys, Paul and Jean, working slowly, completed only three gatherings before Duke Philippe died in April 1404. For a few years he had been living in Paris, often in the *hôtel* of his brother, and Jean de Berry had no doubt seen the Limbourgs and their Bible. He would not have failed to recognize their great promise. Soon after Philippe's death he invited Paul and Jean to work for him and he assigned the *Belles Heures* as their first major commission. Herman, the third brother, apparently joined this enterprise also, as we shall see. We can ascertain these facts about the *Belles Heures* because of its stylistic relationships with both the *Bible moralisée*, documented as the work of Paul and Jean, and the *Très Riches Heures*, which in 1416 the postmortem inventory of the Duke ascribed to "Paul and his brothers." The inventory notice of the *Belles Heures*, written in 1408 or early 1409, is silent about the identity of the authors, probably because the Limbourgs were rather new to the service of Jean de Berry and had not yet acquired a great reputation.

When the manuscript entered the collection it was described by the Duke's incomparable keeper, Robinet d'Estampes.

> Item, unes belles *Heures*, très bien et richement historiées; et au com-
> mancement est le kalendrier, bien richement escript et historié; et après
> est historiée la Vie et Passion de Saincte Katherine; et ensuivant sont
> escriptes les quatre Euvangiles et deux oroisons de Nostre Dame; et
> après commancent les Heures de Nostre Dame, et s'ensuivent pluseurs
> autres heures et oroisons; et au commancement du second fueillet des-
> dictes Heures de Nostre Dame, a escript: *audieritis;* couvertes de veluiau
> vermeil, à deux fermouers d'or, esquielx sont les armes de Monseigneur
> de haulte taille; et par dessus lesdictes Heures a une chemise de veluiau
> vermeil, doublé de satin rouge; lesquelles Heures Monseigneur a fait
> faire par ses ouvriers.

By giving the brothers an appointment and asking them to paint a manuscript Jean de Berry manifested again his inclination to assign pictorial cycles
in books to outstanding or, in this instance, promising artists who practiced,
or had been trained in, other arts. Jacquemart de Hesdin, chief artist of the
Duke's *Brussels Hours*, finished before 1402, probably produced panels or
murals. André Beauneveu, who painted a series of twenty-four prophets and
apostles in the Duke's Psalter, was a leading sculptor. Jean and Herman de
Limbourg served their apprenticeship with a goldsmith, and Paul's art, we
may infer, derived from panel and mural painters as well as from the sculpture of Claus Sluter. It was this series of masters, invited by the Duke to work
in the book, who brought to it qualities of the monumental arts and thus
revolutionized the character of illumination.

The execution of paintings of small size exacted, to be sure, certain
sacrifices; the minute inflections that compose facial expression, for instance,
could less easily be described. This limitation was perhaps willingly accepted
by the Limbourgs, who were not primarily concerned with physiognomy and
the expression of emotion. At times all of them, and most often Herman,
must however have felt hampered. Of course excitement, joy, despair, even
terror, could be readily conveyed by posture and composition, as in the scenes
of the plague (73–74v). Jerome's tension as he listens to a lecture on Plato is
communicated by his crossed arms and the agitation of his drapery (183). The
scale of miniatures did not, however, preclude the recording of the new
analyses of the world of appearance. In this respect some miniatures were,
as a matter of fact, decisively more advanced than panel painting. Their small
size and their private nature, so unlike public monuments, seem to have

stimulated a greater venturesomeness. Often the subjects, too, inspired boldness, and it is certain that illumination offered painters a far wider variety of subjects. The full significance of this opportunity is demonstrated exceptionally well by the diverse themes of the miniatures of the *Belles Heures*, which include not only the more common events of birth, baptism, or death but also speech after death, sexual seduction, and self-mortification.

The decision of the Duke to ask the Limbourgs to undertake a Book of Hours rather than, say, a travel book, conforms with his usual practice of asking the painters in his own service to concern themselves primarily with religious art. Although his collections contained innumerable secular works, including illustrated manuscripts of ancient Roman writers and of ancient mythology and history, he reserved his best illuminators for prayerbooks, above all Books of Hours. Not that his attachment to them was purely pious. Prayer alone and contemplation of the Christian mysteries would scarcely have required an entire series of manuscripts of this kind, even though each painter told the stories in a somewhat different way. The work of Paul de Limbourg in the *Belles Heures*, full of experiments, not to say triumphs, in the solution of problems of form, light, and color, proves that for the Duke as for his painter, aesthetic values were scarcely less important than religious.

The inventories of the Duke describe six exceptionally beautiful Books of Hours, every one of which exists today. They were made over a period of more than thirty years; the last, the *Très Riches Heures*, was unfinished at the Duke's death in 1416.[3] Although at this time Books of Hours tended to follow an established convention, each of the major books of the Duke was given a distinctive character.[4] They range in size from the small *Petites Heures* (21 x 14 cm) to the *Grandes Heures*, a unique giant among Books of Hours (40 x 30 cm). Compared to the latter the *Belles Heures*, which was begun perhaps a year earlier, seems modest in format (23.8 x 17 cm). It is, however, unprecedented in another respect. Each of the seven Penitential Psalms has a miniature, not only, as in most Books of Hours, the first. Similarly, each Hour of the Office of the Passion has not one miniature but two, and Matins has three, all in places reserved for them in the original text. This enthusiasm for extensive illustration is manifested still more strikingly in a unique series of eight picture cycles.

Whereas in a normal Book of Hours miniatures are spaced through the text, falling at the beginning of an Office or an Hour, each of the cycles in the *Belles Heures* consists of a series of miniatures uninterrupted by text. The shortest (the Legend of the Cross) contains three miniatures, the longest (the life of St. Jerome), twelve. Below all but two of the miniatures[5] there are four lines of Latin script, written in a beautiful blue alternating with red. These lines serve as extended titles for the miniatures, although in a few instances the painters, guided by their own visual concerns, failed to maintain a proper correspondence (16v, 18, 74, 94v). The content of these titles is unrelated to the text of a Book of Hours; it was drawn mostly from the *Golden Legend*, an influential compendium of the lives of the saints compiled by Jacobus de Voragine in Italy in the late thirteenth century. At that time there was written in Italy, too, the equally popular *Meditations on the Life of Christ.* Italian artists of the fourteenth century drew imagery from the Latin and Italian texts of this devotional book, and in 1380 the Duke of Berry made it more accessible in a French version to, among others, his painters.[6] Voragine's text, too, was soon translated, and we have consulted a manuscript containing an early fifteenth-century French version.[7]

The special cycles of the *Belles Heures* are thus exceptional in a Book of Hours because of their texts as well as their uninterrupted series of pictures, and all but two of the cycles were, as we shall see, inserted after the book was first designed and much of the text written. The sequences of pictures in the *Belles Heures* are much less characteristic of Books of Hours than of more monumental arts, stained glass, altarpieces, or, especially in Italy, mural cycles in chapels. In France altarpieces or frescoes, originally much fewer in number, have been almost all lost. Some that are mentioned in fourteenth- or early fifteenth-century records may have been iconographically related to miniatures in the *Belles Heures*. These miniatures, however, are demonstrably novel in so many ways that losses alone do not seem to account for the fact that many of them are the earliest surviving examples of their subjects in the whole of Christian art. Thus the eleven scenes of the legend of St. Catherine do not include her vision of the Madonna or her mystical marriage to Christ, an event in her life that, in fourteenth-century Italy at least, began to evoke great interest.[8] The story begins, on the other hand, with the saint quietly reading, devoting herself, as the title says, to the liberal arts (15). This is one of a group of representations in the manuscript concerned with study and teaching.

The second such scene seems likewise to be unprecedented (94). It is centered on a Parisian professor of Holy Writ, Raymond Diocrès, who sits in a large academic *cathedra*, surrounded by monks and clerics. Similar in theme is the miniature of St. Jerome together with other students listening to a lecture on Plato, whose eloquence, the saint confessed, distracted him from Christian writers (183). Jerome soon felt guilty about his enthusiasm for pagan authors, and in a vision represented in the next miniature he saw himself punished by the Lord (183v). Thereafter, as we see, he devoted himself to the translation and revision of the Bible (187v). Except for Jerome in his study, none of these scenes celebrating scholarship and the power of antiquity had been represented earlier; they suggest the influence of the learned men, humanists and theologians, who were members of the Duke of Berry's circle. With an eye on the immediate future, particularly in Renaissance Italy, we may judge these scenes to be the most interesting thematic innovations in the *Belles Heures.*

Since a Book of Hours was intended for private use both the text and illustration of the *Belles Heures* were related to the Duke in other respects also. In addition to two portraits (91, 223v) and the marvelous inscription (1) his armorials were included on five folios (2, 13, 30, 181, 215). On two of these folios, including the *Annunciation* (30), his arms have the form he commonly used before 1405 *(France ancien)*, whereas the other three folios bear *France moderne.* Since two of these are in the calendar (2, 13) we encounter the first suggestion, strongly supported by the style of the miniatures and the borders, that the calendar was, as often in Books of Hours, added late. One of the special cycles—a short one—tells the story of Jean de Berry's name saint, John the Baptist (211-212v). The legend of the recovery of the cross by Heraclius and scenes of the adoration of the cross (156-157) are no doubt connected with one of the Duke's most important relics, a sliver of the True Cross given him by his brother King Charles V, who had sliced it from one of the famous relics still preserved in the Sainte-Chapelle, Paris. Other of these venerated relics appear in scenes of the Passion and of the adoration of the cross (93, 141v, 149, 152, 207v). We know that the Duke patronized the Carthusian Order, the founding of which is described in one of the special cycles (94–97v).

In addition to specific religious interests the Duke and his circle, caught up in the sophisticated society of metropolitan Paris, were doubtless attracted by the simple, austere, contemplative life of the monks. Paintings in the picture cycles devoted to Sts. Anthony and Paul as well as to St. Jerome present a similar eremitic ideal (183-194v). Recent historical events lay behind the choice of the unprecedented cycle of the institution of the Great Litany (73-74v). These prayers, initially offered by Pope Gregory the Great in 590 during an outbreak of plague in Rome, became especially meaningful to Europeans who had lived through the epidemics that had struck periodically since the catastrophic Black Death of 1348.

15

Although some of the innovations of the *Belles Heures*, such as the expanded Passion cycle, were carefully planned before the scribe began to write the text, others were introduced during the course of the work. The five major pictorial cycles in the manuscript—Catherine, the Litany, Diocrès and Bruno, Jerome, Paul and Anthony—are all self-contained, in the sense that they are painted on folios that could have been, and indeed were, inserted into a pre-existing book. Only one of them, the cycle of St. Jerome, is preceded by a rubric that refers to them. This rubric, on 182v, states that the Masses follow, the first devoted to the Birth of Christ, but before them is placed the "vita beati ieronimi tota ystoriata" ("the entire life of the blessed Jerome represented").[9] This unique rubric is not written, however, in the minium or the blue normally used by the scribe for this purpose but in a bluish red—precisely the red used for alternate lines of the script in the titles in the special cycles. The rubric, therefore, was entered at a second stage when the addition of the series of St. Jerome was planned. It does not even then, however, mention the cycle of Sts. Paul and Anthony that follows that of Jerome and that likewise *precedes* the Masses. The story of Paul and Anthony might, therefore, have been added even after this new rubric was written, although its style does not clearly indicate a later date.

The four beautiful scenes of the Great Litany are painted on a bifolio that was slipped into a normal gathering of eight leaves, evidently on second thought (73–74v). Here the make-up of the manuscript strongly confirms our prior judgment that the style of the cycle implies a somewhat later date than that of the miniatures that immediately precede or follow it. The miniatures of St. Catherine, which resemble those of the Great Litany, were also inserted after much of the first part of the text was written. Whereas all the large picture cycles were added to gatherings that had already been written and mostly illuminated, the two similar cycles in the latter part of the book, the Legend of the Cross and of the Baptist, form part of the manuscript as originally designed (156–157, 211–212v). In other words, by the time the scribe came to write the text of the Suffrages and the Masses, the idea of sequences of miniatures had been established and the cycles were incorporated in the original plan. This view of the production and expansion of the *Belles Heures* is supported by the evidence of repetitions in the miniatures to be presented below and by John Plummer's close study of the borders, catchwords, and rubrics—a study he has summarized further on in this book.

The *Belles Heures* continued to grow, then, as it was being made. It is

16

thus entirely unlike illuminated manuscripts produced for the market or destined for the usual kind of purchaser. The important changes and additions are clear signs of the rare combination of an extraordinary patron with no less extraordinary illuminators. The manuscript contains the four readings from the Gospels (22–24), not previously included in the Duke's Books of Hours, and, as a late addition, the Itinerary, not earlier, it seems, illustrated in any Book of Hours (223v). The Penitential Psalms were given seven miniatures instead of the usual one (66–72), and this enthusiasm for pictures was again evinced early—and dramatically—in the exceptionally large Passion cycle (123–152v).

We can establish more firmly our view of the making of the manuscript by observing that several designs and figures in miniatures in the normal illustration of the latter part of the manuscript derive from the special cycles. Jean's *Decapitation of St. Lucy* (179v) is essentially a copy of Paul's *Decapitation of St. Catherine* (19v). In his *Martyrdom of St. Agatha* (179) Jean took his soldier with raised knee and to a degree his saint from his brother's *St. Catherine bound to a column* (17). He found his other soldier in Paul's *St. Catherine before Maxentius* (15v). His Magdalen before Christ on 176v is based on the same brother's St. Catherine on 19v. His priest on 202 recalls Paul's *St. Bruno entering the Chartreuse* on 97. We may infer that two of the inserted cycles, largely by Paul, which are advanced in style and therefore executed late were nevertheless painted before numerous illustrations of the Suffrages and Masses in the last gatherings of the book. This conclusion accords with observations of other kinds made above.

Illustrations were fundamental to the Book of Hours from the time of its initial appearance in France about a century earlier, but no example before the *Belles Heures* had become so fully a picture book. The slightly later *Grandes Heures* of the Duke had far larger miniatures, but with respect to the number and extensiveness of its cycles the *Belles Heures* was unprecedented. Only the *Très Riches Heures* contained a rather comparable series of pictures that told successive episodes in a story. These pictures belong, in fact, to a second stage in the execution of the manuscript, for it underwent changes similar to those of its predecessor. Since neither the *Grandes Heures* nor any other of the Duke's Books of Hours grew similarly we naturally infer that the Limbourgs themselves had a large role in the decision to multiply the paintings, especially by the inclusion of narrative cycles.

The addition of picture cycles was the principal alteration of the *Belles Heures* as the work progressed, but the Limbourgs made a second kind of change—within the picture itself. Several miniatures, for one thing, show pentimenti, implying revisions after the composition was drawn on the vellum. In *Pentecost*, for instance, the golden rays, limited in the finished painting to the central compartment, in Paul's drawing spread to the outer chambers (84). In *Christ nailed to the Cross* a crown of thorns lying on the ground was drawn but not painted (141v). The postures of the Duke (91) and of St. Catherine in her study (15) were altered. These and similar changes to be mentioned presently are signs of the search by the painters for the right form—a search continued up to the final stage of the work.

The Limbourgs, unlike most illuminators, did not wish to fix attention on the borders by filling each of them with its own unique foliage and particular kind of fanciful creature. Furthermore the brothers were not, we recall, trained primarily in the art of illumination. Two of them had been apprenticed to goldsmiths and the genius among them, almost surely to be identified with Paul, learned chiefly from panel painting, Italian as well as French. For him and his brothers it was the pictures that counted. They decreed that, with few exceptions, the borders throughout the manuscript should serve only as broad, sparkling frames for the miniatures. The fine filigree lacks conspicuous, active elements that would distract the eye of the observer from the scene. The three brothers might well have allocated the execution of the borders to more specialized illuminators, as they certainly did for most folios of the *Très Riches Heures*.

To the relative uniformity of the borders of the *Belles Heures* there are, however, a few notable exceptions. The first folio of most of the principal divisions of the manuscript (see p. 25), and of three Suffrages (167, 171, 174), has much richer borders. The first miniature of the Hours of the Virgin, which normally in Books of Hours is especially embellished, has in the *Belles Heures* a uniquely elaborate and very beautiful border (30). Paul, who undoubtedly designed it, introduced large, curling arabesques against a broad band of blue. The leaves form roundels for angels and prophets while nude putti glide along them among the emblems of the Duke: bears, swans, and snails. Except for some less fully developed arabesques in a Parisian Book of Hours dated 1407,[10] this border is the first of its kind. Derived from Italian models, and perhaps specifically from the Porta della Mandorla of the Cathedral of Florence, it was very shortly adopted by the Boucicaut Master and other illuminators in Paris. In gathering eleven and elsewhere small flowers appear alongside the ivy. In gathering four, however, which was probably inserted,

18

and on a few other folios, there are gaps in the ivy, presumably intended for small flowers which never were painted.

The format of most of the miniatures in the *Belles Heures* is rectangular; they are a little higher than wide. The kind of experimentation and change that characterizes the work of the leading painter in the entire book appears in this aspect of it also. When on folio 74 Paul wished to give to Castel Sant' Angelo a greater scale than the normal format would allow he cut away the vines in the upper border to provide space for a rectangular projection. In one early instance, however, *Pentecost* (84), Paul designed a circular top for a high building before the borders were executed. Similar circular projections belong to the initial designs of five miniatures toward the end of the book, for most of which Paul was responsible (161, 174, 211v, 215, 218). To accommodate high forms on 136 and 157 projections were again introduced by erasing part of the border.

By referring to the work of the strongest painter in the *Belles Heures* I have implied distinctions that are discussed in many of the following commentaries, the effect of which will be, I hope, cumulative. From time to time suggestions have been published about differences of style within the *Très Riches Heures*, or even the role in that manuscript of the three brothers of whom the inventory speaks. For the *Belles Heures* no such proposals have ever been offered. Records, furthermore, give us no help. The manuscript was virtually inaccessible until its arrival in the Cloisters and until the appearance, slightly earlier, of a monograph by Jean Porcher, who did not however touch questions of this kind. To solve the problem of authorship we must undertake to do what has not previously been done: broaden the inquiry from one manuscript to all three that survive, and at the same time extract all possible clues from the documents. They enable us, first of all, to discern the style of Paul and of Jean in the Bible datable 1402–1404. The *Belles Heures*, definitely finished in 1408–1409, resembles closely this Bible, and the great painter whom we first meet on certain pages of that book is surely also the author of the best miniatures in the *Belles Heures*. His strength makes him the most readily identifiable. It is nevertheless true that in the *Belles Heures* we encounter him at different moments and in different moods.

In the miniatures in the Hours of the Virgin, probably his first in the manuscript, Paul was seeking to develop further his blend of Northern visual intimacy in the depiction of nature with Italian modes of figural articulation and geometric design. His growing mastery of the principles of Tuscan painting is demonstrated by the *Nativity*, with its pointing shepherd and large rectangles or trapezoids (48v). The Tuscan repertory of postures and gestures is the ultimate source of his grave, revolving Virgin in the *Annunciation* (30). For the *Lamentation* (149v) and *Entombment* (152) he took a dramatic figure from Simone Martini, and for the *Flight* (63) a soaring angel from Giotto or a follower. This latter borrowing, together with clear signs of the study of the work of Altichiero and his circle, suggest a visit to Padua and Florence before the beginning of the *Belles Heures*. This phase of Paul's work seems to culminate in the *Flight*, in which powerful, gyrating volumes are cloaked in varied textures and displayed in a soft, pervasive light (63).

This most advanced of the miniatures in the Hours of the Virgin comes close to the picture cycle that, somewhat later, was inserted before it, the story of St. Catherine (15–20). Perhaps the most impressive of the ventures of various kinds Paul undertook in this cycle is a blond palette of unprecedented hues. He quickly recognized, furthermore, the several opportunities offered by an uninterrupted series of paintings and sometimes designed facing folios to correspond, in color as well as in design. Thus the compositions of 18v, 19 are related and the colors of 15v, 16 are similar but reversed. Conceiving the pictorial space to be independent of the frame and continuous behind it he boldly painted buildings of which only a part is visible (16, 17v). The landscape of Mt. Sinai, in which nestles the diminutive monastery, has a remarkable scale (20). These representations imply a deeper understanding of perspective, and this Paul applied to the figures also, giving them strongly foreshortened postures entirely new to Northern art and uncommon even in Italy (18v, 19). These postures serve to intensify the illusion of space and to create a highly dramatic effect. He employed them again, for similar purposes, in the cycles of the Litany and the Passion (73v, 74, 149v).

The form Paul gave to the monastery of St. Catherine (20) represents a departure from the medieval principle of denoting a building by depiction of a characteristic feature, for his structure approximates the actual appearance of the monastery in its wild and dramatic setting. The Grande Chartreuse is similarly conceived (97v), and indeed the picture of the monastery in its mountainous setting is unaccompanied by a religious episode and constitutes the principal theme—an innovation in its time and the precursor of the calendar pictures in the *Très Riches Heures*. In the *Itinerary*, too, Paul may have represented a specific Burgundian chateau (223v). In the cycle of the Litany, however, Castel Sant'Angelo (74) bears some, but much less, resemblance to the building in Rome; perhaps it looks so domestic because of the

French painter's ignorance. Nevertheless Paul gave it an appropriate scale, even at the cost of extending the miniature over the upper border after it had been painted.

The cycle of the Great Litany is no less memorable for its luminous color—indeed in this respect these miniatures constitute a landmark in the history of color, and they remained unique in Paul's work (73–74v). He did not find these hues in the paint pots of his contemporaries and predecessors. The glistening enamels of his time probably offered suggestions, and he surely responded no less warmly than the Duke to the latter's unrivaled collection of precious stones. Paul must have looked intently also at another of nature's displays of color: flowers; one suspects, however, that even the Duke's gardener never dreamt of combinations like those in the most ravishing miniatures. The painter's brush transformed even tombstones into a floral bouquet (95). His exquisite modulations of blue disclose the exceptional sensitiveness to this color in France, manifested already in stained glass windows and still today one of the delights of French clothing and even billboards. Perhaps even rarer is Paul's mastery of white. The Flagellants (74v) and the Carthusians (97) precede the marvelous snowscape in the *Très Riches Heures*.

The contributions to the *Belles Heures* of its greatest painter emerge quite clearly, it seems to me, but what of the other miniatures? In extant documents all three brothers appear in the service of the Duke only in 1411, two or three years after the *Belles Heures* was completed. We thus cannot assume that every one of them worked on the *Belles Heures*, nor if they did, *how* they worked. Were the miniatures simply divided among the artists in the usual manner? Or did they, like some other major painters and illuminators, collaborate more closely, occasionally contributing to the same small picture?

For questions of such great difficulty the documents that help us to identify the style of two brothers, Paul and Jean, in the Bible enable us to find them at a slightly later date in the *Belles Heures*. But what of Herman? I finally discovered him only by recognizing that a third group of miniatures in the manuscript, the least accomplished as a matter of fact, are earlier paintings by one of the three brothers who worked, the inventory tells us, on the *Très Riches Heures*. The largest and most distinctive group of miniatures in the *Belles Heures* in this style is in the Passion cycle (123v–145v). The figures are weakly structured, and compositional movement tends to be generated less by them than by the design as a whole. The masculine faces are assertive and dour, and they, like all the forms, show strong contrasts of light and dark as well as of warm and cool colors. Among all the miniatures in the book the paintings of Herman are the most demonstrative; they verge on the melodramatic. Paul, as we have seen, was the most perceptive, the most thoughtful, and the most deeply ambitious. Jean was the most lyrical, the most elegant, and the most variable.

The commentaries that follow contain many additional observations on these three styles, although for some miniatures, usually inferior artistically, I have so far been able to offer no solution worth recording. The three styles are frequently quite distinctive but occasionally they interpenetrate, as in the instances already noted of the adoption by Jean of figures by Paul. Herman, too, sometimes depended similarly on Paul (142). We shall refer, furthermore, to entire scenes which were painted by Jean or Herman on drawings furnished, we believe, by Paul (94). In compositions Paul designed he usually painted the principal figures, but he sometimes left the others to Jean or Herman (15v, 16v, 18, 19, 152, 161). In one miniature he painted the building but Jean, it seems, the figures (223v). The leading painter was not, however, above adding a figure or two to a miniature painted by one of his collaborators (123v, 142, 156v). As in the *Très Riches Heures* Jean was apparently judged the right master to portray the Duke, either alone or among companions (91, 223v).

In 1410, a year or two after the completion of the *Belles Heures*, the Duke gave Paul a house. Whereas princes frequently provided their artisans with dwellings, Paul's was highly exceptional. A royal order of 1434 described it as one of the largest and most impressive houses in Bourges, suitable for a nobleman of the blood—"bien propre pour logier l'un des seigneurs de nostre sang. . . ." Paul and his wife (the daughter of a rich local merchant) thus lived in an unprecedented manner, less like a contemporary craftsman than in the style of Mantegna at the court of the Gonzaga or Raphael in papal Rome. The Duke continued to show his delight with the work of Paul and his brothers by gifts of gold coins and precious stones, and they reciprocated with less costly objects. Once they even lent the Duke a large sum of money—against security. One of the gifts of the painters illuminates vividly their capacity for deceptive realism, their full awareness of their patron's enthusiasms, and their wit: they gave the most passionate collector of illuminated manuscripts in history a fake book, painted on wood and covered with white velvet.

The financial security, not to say wealth, enjoyed by the Limbourgs fostered, especially in the instance of Paul, an exceptional awareness of his creative powers. He was, he knew, producing paintings greatly appreciated by the most discriminating patron in Europe. He no doubt recognized also a novel opportunity to concentrate on problems of form, on the telling of the traditional stories in new ways. He and his brothers studied with unprecedented intensity the appearance of the world around them. They had both the time and the means to go to Italy for a fuller understanding of the radically new painting than could be obtained from the limited number of examples visible in French collections. In the *Belles Heures*, as a result, Paul achieved a balance between Trecento idealism and descriptive naturalism that was to remain, in Europe as a whole, peculiarly French.

In these attitudes and achievements Paul resembled the painters of Quattrocento Italy more than his predecessors in the North. The greater concern with formal problems, the value of originality and individual style, the awareness of a new social esteem—these are the hallmarks of Italian art of the fifteenth century. Italian painters at this time, furthermore, gave especial attention to light and perspective—both central concerns of Paul. To these similarities with early Renaissance artists we may add the association of the brothers with learned men in the Duke's circle; to them they owed some understanding of intellectual life and an awareness of history and of ethnic and cultural differences. Out of this knowledge they shaped such scenes as the story of the cross and of the burial of St. Catherine on Mount Sinai. Under the influence of the scholars they painted miniatures of Sts. Catherine and Jerome engaged in study, or the latter at a lecture on Plato.

Although nothing is gained by claiming that the *Belles Heures* is a "Renaissance phenomenon," neither is it, in its most beautiful and adventurous aspects, a work of the International or Courtly Style. Paul, and to a lesser extent his brothers, hold an even more important place in European painting than has hitherto been awarded them, and the *Belles Heures*, along with the *Boucicaut Hours*, is the most impressive group of paintings produced in Europe in the first decade of the fifteenth century—just as the *Très Riches Heures* is in the second. Paul's color anticipates the colorists of the second quarter of the century in Italy—Fra Angelico, Uccello, Domenico Veneziano, Piero della Francesca—and perhaps it was somehow even known to them. They in turn provided models—everyone agrees—for the next group of French painters, Quarton, Fouquet, and the René Master. These French masters, however, may have had direct knowledge of the *Belles Heures* itself; at the death of the Duke it was bought by the eminent Duchess of Anjou, mother-in-law of King Charles VII, so that the manuscript could have been seen at her court or at his.

Thus in one way or another Paul's luminous color in his earlier book entered the mainstream of fifteenth-century painting. In the *Très Riches Heures* his coloristic pattern served more completely other compositional purposes, and as its autonomy was reduced so was its originality.

Historical considerations aside, the color of the Catherine and Litany cycles is a great delight. Since it appears in a manuscript and has been protected over the centuries from light and abrasion it is almost perfectly preserved. It has a virtually complete authenticity, uncommon in panel and mural painting. Anyone who wishes to measure the significance of this freshness may compare works by the same artist in both media when, as rarely, they happen to survive: a panel, for example, in the Metropolitan Museum (New York) by the early fifteenth-century Lombard master Michelino da Besozzo and the pages painted by him in a Book of Hours nearby in the Pierpont Morgan Library.

Not long after the completion of the *Belles Heures* color began to be immersed in darker shadows. Jan van Eyck developed the new mode of painting in the North, and in Italy late in the fifteenth century Leonardo da Vinci created his shadowy world. Leonardo apparently recognized, however, what losses his deep hues entailed.

> Every color is more beautiful in the light than in shadow, because light enlivens and gives a true perception of the quality of color, while shadow deadens and darkens this same beauty and clouds perception of the color *[Treatise on Painting].*[11]

To us, taught by the sunny scenes of the Impressionists and the bright canvases of Matisse, the clear color of the *Belles Heures* strikes a familiar—and memorable—chord.

Principal Groups of Miniatures
in the Belles Heures

Note on the Plates

The folios are reproduced in actual size, except for slight trimming around the outer edges. The 127 miniatures reproduced in color appear, of course, in their actual sequence in the manuscript. The remaining thirty miniatures in the manuscript, generally less important, appear in black and white in the back of the book.

Miniatures that face one another always preserve that relationship on the pages of this book. All folios reproduced in color retain their precise places in the manuscript, whether recto or verso. All but a few commentaries (80, 155, 218) precede or face the miniature they describe.

Plates and Commentaries

Fol. 1   Ex-libris of Jean de Berry.

Both the father of Jean de Berry, King Jean le Bon, and his brother, King Charles V, formed libraries of manuscripts and, like them, the Duke normally wrote his ex-libris at the end of the text. We are not surprised that so discerning a connoisseur wrote in a fine hand. His signature, not written in the *Belles Heures,* contained two capitals of the kind then charmingly called *cadeaux.* Elaborate as they seem, they pale beside those of his secretary on the opposite page.

In a few of his most prized illuminated books Jean de Berry himself did not enter his ex-libris but asked his secretary, Jean Flamel, to write a more splendid one at the beginning. Flamel developed in an extraordinary way the ornamental script traditionally used in charters. His flamboyant capitals burst into marvelous serifs, freer in their flow than the related vines of the borders. Even the minuscules shoot out astonishing appendages, and indeed the character of a letter is greatly determined by its place in the stream. The folio seems alive with—one has only musical terms—trills, arpeggios, and a cadenza. Flamel's ex-libris are unique in their time.

The inscription reads:

Ces heures fist faire tres excellent et puissant Prince Jehan—filz de Roy de France —Duc de Berry et Dauvergne Conte de Poitou destampes de Bouloingne et dauvergne. Flamel.

(This Book of Hours was made at the wish of the most excellent and powerful Prince John—son of the King of France—Duke of Berry and of Auvergne, Count of Poitou, of Estampes, of Boulogne, and of Auvergne. Flamel.)

Les Heurs fist faire Er

Excellent et Puissant Prince Jehan

Filz de Roy de France. Duc de Berry

Et d'auvergne Conte de Poitou d'estampes

De Boulongne Et d'auvergne. Lamet

The text of the calendar for each of the twelve months begins on a recto and ends on a verso which lacks miniatures. January and December have especially rich borders, including the Duke's arms.

An old and somewhat variable tradition of illustration had established certain actions, tasks, or pleasures as typical of the months. In the *Belles Heures* this scene is represented in a quatrefoil at the head of each page and the zodiacal sign appears beneath.

The new year began then as it does now with drinking and feasting. In the *Belles Heures* the transition from old to new year is symbolized by the Roman deity of portals, of beginnings and endings, Janus the two-faced, who has given his name to the month. An old and a young man sit back to back. The youth raises a yellow cup whereas his older companion has emptied his—it is cool violet—and he stretches out a hand, probably in vain, toward a pitcher.

In the lower quatrefoil Aquarius, the zodiacal sign of the month, spills water from his heavy jug by tilting it in a complex and original movement. A sturdy figure, he leans down and sideways, bracing himself with an arm on his hip and with widely spread legs. He is given support of another kind by the frame of the quatrefoil, which encloses his jug and stabilizes his two feet. The transparent water splashing on the floor forms a beautiful, quasi-geometric pattern.

In all these forms we encounter for the first time in the manuscript the mastery of the greatest of the three brothers, Paul. We do not see him, however, at the beginning of his work on the manuscript but at the end, for, as we have said in the Introduction, the calendar was one of the last sections to be painted.

As a member of the royal family and a resident of Paris, Jean de Berry followed the use of Paris; the church calendar therefore includes not only the universal feasts but those peculiar to the capital. They are listed throughout in alternate lines of blue and red, whereas feasts of major importance were written in gold. The Duke's shield and the emblem that bears it, the swan, appear over the bird's proper element, rippling blue water. The decision to introduce it here might well have taken into account the fact that water is equally appropriate to the zodiacal sign of the month.

Januier a xxix. iour.

Et la lune xxix.

iij. La circoncision. S. eg.

b Kl' Octaues s esthêne
xi. c Kl' sainte geneuieue.
d Kl' Oct des innocens.
xix. e Nõs sainct symeon.
vuj. f id' La typhaine.
g id' saint franont.
b id' sainct lucien.
v. b id' saint pol hmite.
c id' saint guille.
xuij. d id' saint saueur.
ij. e id' saint laur.
f id' saint hylaire.
x. g Kl' saint felir.
Kl' saint mor

Eustache Deschamps, a French poet of the late fourteenth century, wrote verses on the terrible cold of deep winter indoors, even in the royal palace. Combating it had long been a typical scene in illustrations of the months. Here an elderly man, his head muffled in a hood under a black fur hat, sits warming his hands before the fire. Flames leap up and smoke escapes into the room from under the mantel over the fireplace—an astonishing representation at this early date. The two long, narrow objects roasting before the fire may represent jocularly the zodiacal sign of the month, Fishes. They are painted on a larger scale, and brilliantly, below.

The structure within which the man tries to keep warm looks like a stage set, with the huge fireplace balanced by a rectangular building, as green as the fish below. A considerable depth is created by the receding planes and lines, especially by the converging lines of the tan ceiling and floor. Even more advanced than the perspective is the extension of the building beyond the frame. One has the impression of seeing, as through a window, only a small part of a large structure—a novel effect that was not equaled until some years later, even in Italy.

feurier a xxviij. iours.
Et la lune xxx.

	d		sainte brude.
ij.	e	N.	la chandeleur.
xix.	f	N.	saint blaise.
viij.	g	N.	saint auentin.
	A	Nõs	sainte agate.
xbj.	b	iő	saint amant.
v.	c	iő	sainte helenne.
	d	iő	saint salomon.
xiij.	e	iő	sainte apoline.
ij.	f	iő	sainte scolastique.
	g	iő	saint desier.
x.	A	iő	sainte eulalie.
	b	idus	saint lucien.
xbiij.	c	kl.	saint ualentin
vij.	d	kl.	saint maurel. Sol in pisab.

In March the soil begins to thaw and peasants till the leafless vines, before a luminous "sky" of finely tooled gold leaf. A gray-haired but barefooted man in a tattered yellow smock breaks the earth with his hoe. His companion, leaning on his staff under the weight of a basket of rich brown manure, dumps it around the roots. He moves like the Water-carrier in January (2). Like that figure, too, he is "locked" into the frame. The low posture of his powerful companion, who has bent down close to the ground, is compensated in this design by a hill behind. These are all signs of Paul's taste and, indeed, proof of his mastery. No painter of the time, furthermore, rendered men at work so sympathetically.

Aries is a splendid ram with a long tail, curly fleece, and curving horns. The clear blue-green of the horns and of the ground on which the animal stands, set off by deep blue and white, has all the usual subtlety of Paul's patterns of color.

Mars a xxxi. iour.
Et la lune xxx.

iij.	d		saint aubin.
	e	N̄.	saint prune
xi.	f	N̄.	saint maurin.
	g	N̄.	saint andrien
xix.	A	N̄.	saint sarurin.
viij	b	N̄.	sainte felice.
	c	Nōs	saint thomas daquin.
xvj.	d	id̄	sainte potenciane.
v.	e	id̄	saint loutoul.
	f	id̄	saint alixandre.
xiij.	g	id̄	saint blanchart.
ij.	A	id̄	saint gregoire.
	b	id̄	saint lubin.
x.	c	id	saint innocent
	d	idus	Saint longin.

Fol. 5 April. Taurus (The Bull). JEAN OR HERMAN

Spring is the traditional season for courting and here a young nobleman carrying a green branch pauses as he crosses the meadow to smell the flower he has plucked from the blossoming fruit trees. This courtier, unlike the powerful figures in the first three months, seems relatively flat and disjointed. He is, however, very elegant, with his wide-brimmed hat and fur-lined tunic. Here for the first time we find a change of subject accompanied by a change of style and of artist.

The gold ground in this and preceding quatrefoils is finely tooled in the manner of an associate of the Limbourgs, the Master of the Breviary of Jean sans Peur. In our opinion he did the same kind of work in the *Très Riches Heures,* and he may well have been responsible for these tooled backgrounds in the *Belles Heures,* which occur only in the calendar. Since the calendar was painted late, his collaboration with the Limbourgs would have begun in it and then continued two or three years later when the *Très Riches Heures* was undertaken.

Although the bull shares the flatness of the nobleman and was probably painted by the same illuminator Paul seems to have provided the model. The lively animal, lashing its tail and lowering its horns, would be as much at home in Paul's freshly observed natural world as in the realm of conventional zodiacal symbols.

Auril a xxx. iours.
Et la lune. xxix.
saint ualeri.
vi. saint egipciene.
b saint pancrace.
xix. c saint ambroise.
vuj. d Noz sainte yrarne
xvi. e id' saint thimothe
v. f id' saint macaire
g id' sainte apoline
xuj id' saint procor.
ii. b id' saint gobert.
c id' saint lyon
x. d id' saint marcel.
e id' saint yfame.
xvuj. f id' saint ualerien
vij. g kl'. saint presme

Fol. 6   May. Gemini (The Twins).

JEAN OR HERMAN

Riding a sturdy white horse caparisoned in blue to match his tunic, a young man goes hawking with his falcon perched on his wrist. The nobles traditionally celebrated May Day by riding out into the countryside carrying green branches and wearing wreaths of green leaves.

Because the constellation of Gemini is composed of the twin stars Castor and Pollux the zodiacal sign is usually represented by two male figures. Here, however, the heavenly twins are deliberately disparate. Not only are they male and female, brunette and blonde, but she is even the taller of the two. The painter has avoided the problems of entire nakedness by providing them with a beautiful yellow and orange shield.

In contrast to Paul's quatrefoils these figures by Jean or Herman are nowhere overlapped by the frame; rather their heads and feet extend slightly over it.

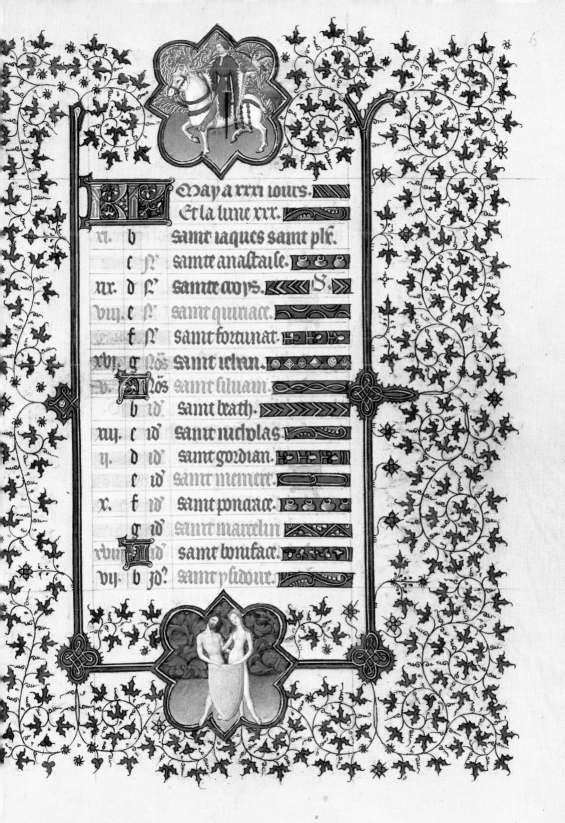

May a xxxi iours.
Et la lune xxx.

xi.	b		saint iaques saint plc̄.
	c	f̄	sainte anastaise.
xix.	d	f̄	saintceroys.
vij.	e	f̄	saint quiriace.
	f	f̄	saint fortunat.
xbj.	g	ñōs	saint iehan.
b.	A	ñōs	saint siluain.
	b	id'	saint beath.
xiij.	c	id'	saint nicolas.
ij.	d	id'	saint gordian.
	e	id'	saint memert.
x.	f	id'	saint ponace.
	g	id'	saint marcelin.
xbiij.	A	id'	saint boniface.
vij.	b	id?	saint plidoine.

For the season of haymaking a peasant scythes the high grass. Within his small compass the painter has created a powerful illusion of a hillside in a wider landscape. By differences of color and brush-stoke he contrasts cut swaths and the standing grass. He was eager to realize not only extended spaces and imposing volumes but foreshortened planes as well. Since he was only beginning to explore perspective the tilted straw hat covers the worker's face so completely that he apparently cannot see what he is doing. Paul partly solved this problem when he designed his reapers for *June* and *July* in the *Très Riches Heures*. In general the figure in the *Belles Heures* resembles one in *July*, whereas it is superior to those in *June*, which Paul himself did not execute. It is fascinating to see how much these very small scenes in the *Belles Heures* anticipate the calendar pictures of the *Très Riches Heures*.

The unusually large Cancer breaks out of its frame, its long antennae stretching across the folio. It looks, indeed, less like the conventional sign of the crab than a real, live lobster.

Juing a .xxx. iours.
Et la lune .xxix.

	e		saint nicomede.
xix.	f	N	saint marcellin.
viij.	g	N	saint liessart.
xvj.		N	saint pontalin
v.	b	Nõs	saint bonisace
	c	id	saint ponce.
xiij.	d	id	saint proiet
ij.	e	id	saint medart.
	f	id	saint seliaen.
x.	g	id	saint landri
		id	saint barnabe
xviij	b	id	saint basilide
vij.	c	id	sainte feriule.
	d	kl	saint vistin.
xv.	e	kl	saint modest.

The peasants work on what is clearly a warm, sunny summer day. In all the innumerable depictions of the labors of the months no artist before Paul had conveyed so vividly the temperature and the quality of light of the season. The harvesters wear thin white shirts, beautifully luminous before the light green grass and the ripe yellow wheat. One hat is yellow, the other Paul's characteristic pale gray.

The harvesters have paused in their reaping to bind the wheat into sheaves. One pulls the cut stalks together with his sickle, another kneels on the sheaf as he draws the binding tight. The quatrefoil, as in other miniatures by Paul, acts as a window opening on to a much wider scene. The tip of a foot, part of the kneeling figure, uncut wheat, stalks lying loose in the foreground—all extend behind the frame. This detachment of the composition from the quatrefoil is, however, accompanied by the geometric and rhythmical interrelations between them that we have seen in preceding miniatures by Paul. Here one leg is on the central vertical axis, an arm on the central horizontal one. The zigzag of the kneeling peasant corresponds to the triangle of the frame. The nearer peasant moves to the right of center, the sheaf behind him to the left. All the forms are thus charged with many values. The miniature is a little masterpiece.

The sun now enters the sign of Leo, which is represented here as a heraldic lion passant, with his tail curling back against delicate gold fronds.

Juillet a xxxi. iours.
Et la lune. xxix.

xix.	f		saint tibaut
viij.	g	iiij	saint piars
	b	iij	saint appolin.
xvi.	c	ij	saint martin.
v.	d	ij	saint donnique
	e	ij	Oct. saint pierre & pol.
xiij.	f	Nõs	saint thomas.
ij.	g	id	saint claude
		id	saint zenon.
x.	b	id	les .vij. freres.
	c	id	saint benoit.
xviij	d	id	saint sist
vij.	e	id	saint wistin.
	f	id	saint naalt.
xv.	g	id	saint florentin.

Fol. 9   August. Virgo (The Virgin).   PAUL AND JEAN OR HERMAN

The harvest ends with threshing. August is not as bright as July. The scanty clothing of the peasant assures us, however, of continued heat. Indeed as he lifts his flail high to beat the grain his shirt flies back and exposes his rotund belly.

Once again part of the principal figure coincides with the central vertical axis of the miniature, and the grain is arranged in an interesting geometric pattern. The powerful figure was surely designed by Paul, but in execution it and the entire miniature do not quite equal the painter's best.

Virgo, evidently painted by Jean or Herman, holds the palm of a virgin saint in one hand and a leafy branch in the other.

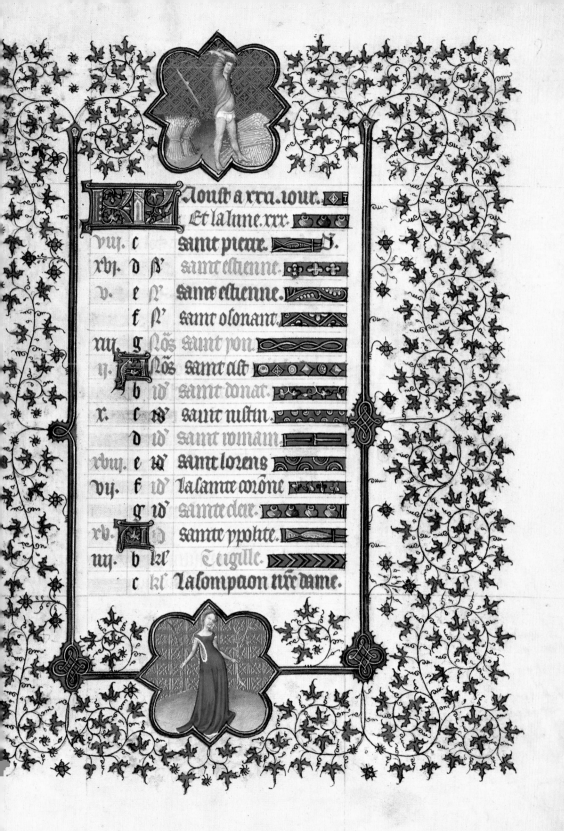

Aoust a xxxi. iour.
Et la lune. xxx.

vij.	c		saint pierre.	ij.
xbj.	d	ij	saint estienne.	
v.	e	ij	saint estienne.	
	f	ij	saint olonant.	
xiij.	g	Nos	saint pon.	
ij.	A	Nos	saint ast.	
	b	id	saint donat.	
x.	c	ib	saint nistin.	
	d	id	saint romain.	
xbiij.	e	ib	saint lorens	
vij.	f	id	la sainte corône	
	g	id	sainte clare.	
xb.	A	id	sainte yppolite.	
iiij.	b	kl	Teigille.	
	c	kl	la sompaon nře dame.	

September is still warm but not bright. The vintage is the traditional subject, and here a peasant pours a hod full of grapes into the vat to be trodden by a fellow worker, nude except for a brief loincloth.

In contrast to these strong peasants an elegant young woman holds the scales, representing Libra. She is dressed fashionably in a deep blue gown, lifted in front to show the white lining. The horizon coincides exactly with the line of the frame, dividing the space equally between the greensward and the lively background of gold leaf, again finely worked to reflect the light. A precise, simple compositional division of this kind does not conform with Paul's taste. Even in the work of his brothers, one of whom painted this miniature, it is uncommon. Could it, like the scales, convey the idea of an exact balance?

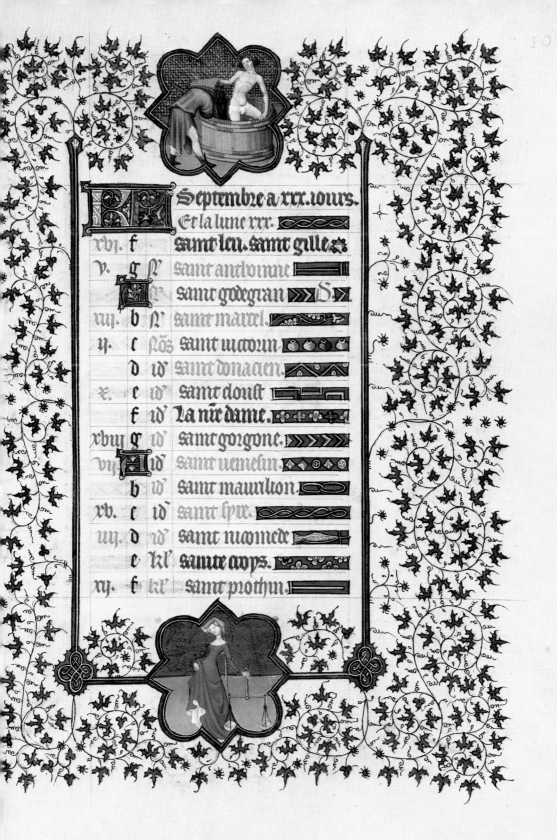

KL Septembre a xxx. iours.
Et la lune xxx.

xbj.	f		saint leu. saint gille.
v.	g	N̄	saint anthoine
	iij	N̄	saint godegran
xiij.	b	N̄	saint martel
y.	c	Iđs	saint nicenin
	d	iđ	saint donacien
x.	e	iđ	saint clouст
	f	iđ	La nře dame.
xbiij.	g	iđ	saint gorgone.
vij.	**A**	iđ	saint nemelin.
	b	iđ	saint maurilion
xb.	c	iđ	saint syre.
iiij.	d	iđ	saint nicomede
	e	kł	sainte crops.
xij.	f	kł	saint prothin.

Summer is over, the fields have been plowed, and long furrows in the rich brown earth await the winter seed. The sower, a ruddy peasant not quite steady on his feet, scatters the seed held in his apron. Even in their earliest work, the *Bible moralisée*, the Limbourgs had shown an exceptional interest in describing tools and techniques. Here Paul, who probably designed the miniature but left the painting to Herman, has introduced a triangular harrow and, in the sack, a wooden scoop for the grain. In Herman's manner the colors are deeper and more opaque, and the mosaic in the background is more dense.

The scorpion, opaque, compact, and rather small within the quatrefoil, seems to be entirely Herman's. In northern Europe he would scarcely have seen this creature alive, but he and his brothers were no doubt familiar with astrological manuscripts and in the *Belles Heures* it was provided, quite correctly, with a pair of nipping claws and a flexible tail with a sting.

Octobre a xxxi. iour.

Et la lune xxx.

xbi	a	kl	saint Remi.
v.	b	iiii	saint ligier
xiii.	c	iii	saint victor.
iii.	d	ii	saint francoys.
	e	ii	sainte cristine.
x.	f	ii	sainte foy.
	g	Nõs	saint marc.
xbiii	A	id'	saint demetrir.
bi.	b	id'	saint denis
	c	id'	saint gerion.
xb.	d	id'	la traslacion S. augustin.
iiii.	e	id'	saint venant
	f	id'	saint aurien.
xii.	g	id'	saint calixte.
i.	A	id'	saint offian.

Fol. 12   November. Sagittarius (The Archer).   JEAN ?

A swineherd providing for his pigs is the traditional scene for November. He takes an easy course, simply knocking acorns from the oaks, although in reality they would be higher and less accessible than the pictorial conventions of the period show them in the miniature.

Like the courtier smelling his flower in April, the peasant who leans back to cast his stick is not well put together. The illuminator who painted both miniatures, perhaps Jean, is less interested in bodily structure than in the decorative pattern of a sleeve and hood against the surface of the gold. As in other miniatures in the calendar the gold is given greater sparkle by minute punctures which form curving lines.

Sagittarius has the body of a goat, quite similar to the centaur encountered by St. Anthony (192). Wearing a hat to shield his eyes, the Archer bounds forward, turning to dispatch an arrow in his flight.

			Nouembre a .xxx. iours.
			Et la lune xxx.
	d		la tous sains.
xiɣ.	e	N̄	les mors.
ɣ.	f	N̄	saint marcel.
	g	N̄	saint dier.
x.	A	Nōs.	saint ye.
	b	iđ	saint lienart.
xbiɣ.	c	iđ	saint herculain.
bɣ.	d	iđ	les .iiɣ. coronnes.
	e	iđ	saint mathelin.
xb.	f	iđ	saint uerain.
iiɣ.	g	iđ	saint martin.
	A	iđ	saint leonin.
xɣ.	b	idus	saint brice.
.i.	c	kł	saint eugene.
	d	kł	saint madou.

The calendar ends as it began, with a rich border which includes the Duke's arms. This time both of his emblems—the bear and the swan—are present and a scroll displays his motto, *le temps van[dra]* (*the time will come*). The small brown bears are more lively than the usual heraldic supporters. On one side, beneath the spread wings of the swan, they have neatly centered the shield and hold it upright. Their more playful fellows are either still struggling to put it in place or one has pushed the shield and almost tumbled his partner backwards.

The slaughter of a boar is the most vigorous composition of all the works of the months. The powerful peasant, twisting and swaying, poises his axe for the blow. Three salient vertical folds of his white garment establish the axis around which he turns. Man, beast, and golden frame are closely related in a rhythmical pattern of curves. Even the skyline, lifted toward the left, seems to reinforce the power of the stroke.

Unlike the swine of November the boar is no docile farmyard beast. He arches his spine, bristles grow out of his hairy sides, his tusks are extremely sharp, and the whites of his eyes seem menacing. Nevertheless he lies still, close to the ground, and turns his head as if to find refuge in the lobe of the frame.

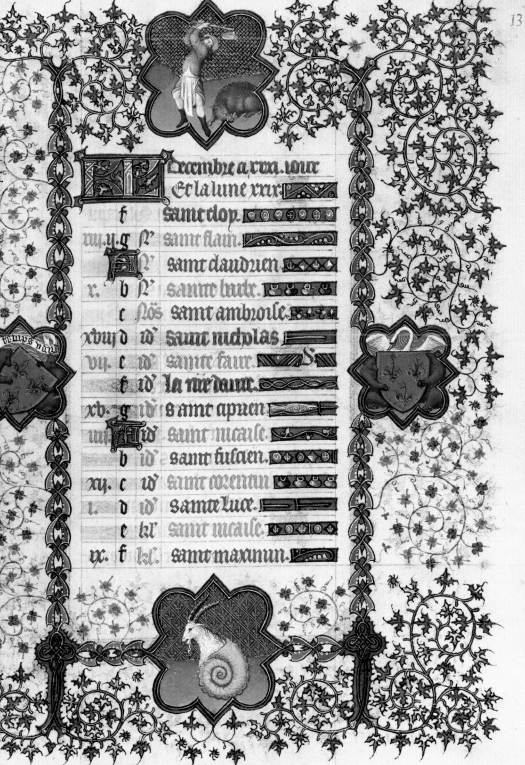

Decembre a .xxxi. iour
Et la lune xxix.

	f		saint eloy.
xiiij.y.	g	l'	sainte flaur.
		N'	saint claudien
x.	b	N'	sainte barbe.
	c	Nõs	saint ambroise.
xbiij	d	iv'	saint nicholas
vij.	e	id'	sainte faure.
	f	id'	la nre dame.
xb.	g	id'	saint apuen
iiij		id'	saint nicaise.
	b	id'	saint fuscien.
xij.	c	iv'	saint corentin
i.	d	id'	sainte luce.
	e	kl'	saint nicaise.
ix.	f	kl.	saint maximin.

Catherine, daughter of King Costus, versed in all including the liberal arts [and] of incredible beauty, the admiration of all eyes, became celebrated in Alexandria, a city of Egypt, in the time of the Emperor Maxentius.

The four lines of text below the miniature on the facing page were, like most of the titles below miniatures in the picture cycles, taken from the *Golden Legend*. The Latin is greatly abbreviated, elliptical, and not free of errors; our translation is often not literal but gives what we take to be its gist.

Of the eight cycles in the *Belles Heures* the first and one of the longest (eleven scenes) tells the story of St. Catherine of Alexandria. Her remarkable prominence is maintained in the miniature of All Saints on 218. Catherine was one of the saints especially venerated by the Valois, and because she was, as the *Golden Legend* says, "born in the purple," many royal ladies, including the Duke's wife Jeanne de Boulogne (represented on 91v), placed themselves under her protection. The title tells us that Catherine was "versed in all including the liberal arts," and consequently she was chosen as patroness of scholars and of the University of Paris.

The first scene is unprecedented and may, indeed, be unique. The beautiful daughter of King Costus sits quietly reading in a large interior that, as in earlier Italian paintings, is visible through an "entrance arcade." Like the Duchess on 91v she has the long slender neck, sloping shoulders, blond hair, and pale complexion of a contemporary aristocratic beauty. The stand near her holds two circular tiers of exquisitely bound books. On top appears Moses, the recipient of the Ten Commandments and so to speak the publisher of them. He represents the written word, and, furthermore, he received the Law on the peak of Sinai next to the one on which angels buried St. Catherine. Moses is represented again—this time without the usual horns—as a statue on the altar of a chapel. Near the foot of the mountain the Lord spoke to him from the Burning Bush, and on that site, later within the church of St. Catherine, a chapel was dedicated to him. The chapel in the miniature may well allude to this structure, especially because the building around St. Catherine, with its large clerestory window, might refer to her church.

Close examination discloses that the painter modified slightly his design of the saint's head. Originally it was turned more toward the beholder and downward.

Katherina costi regis filia oim q̃: liberaliū arti
um studijs erudita et mirabili pulc̃ritudiẽ
omniū oculis admirablis ĩ alexandria ciui
tate egypti tẽpoze naxceą imperatozis claruit

Fol. 15v   St. Catherine refuses to worship an Idol.   PAUL AND JEAN

Catherine, a virgin of eighteen years, learning that the Emperor Maxentius was obliging Christians to sacrifice to idols on pain of death, armed with the sign of the cross, confounded him at the temple gate with the depth of her remarkable learning and her eloquence.

Catherine expounds the Christian faith to the Emperor and seeks to persuade him that the golden statue of Mars on a column between them represents the false gods. She is much less closely associated with the idol than he. She extends two fingers of her right hand as if to make the sign of the cross and she is armed with a book. The Emperor, unable to match her in dispute, brandishes a sword and turns to consult with an officer. It seems possible that while Paul de Limbourg designed the miniature and probably painted the two protagonists some or all figures in the group at the right were executed by his brother Jean.

Catherine stands alone, in a smaller space than her adversaries. She remains the dominant figure because of her breadth, her movement, and the contrast of her spreading blue mantle and white tunic with the Emperor's paler hues. The unusual color combinations of mustard against violet and soft sage-green over rose accord closely with other miniatures in the cycle. The range of hue differs from that in the following miniatures in the Hours of the Virgin, and, as we have remarked in the Introduction, the Catherine cycle was painted later during the work on the book and then inserted in its present place.

Fol. 16   St. Catherine confounding the Doctors.   PAUL

Catherine, a virgin, by her reasoning confounds fifty philosophers and rhetors summoned by the Emperor from afar, and, turning them from the errors of idols, converts them to Christ; the Emperor casting them into the fire [confers on them] the crown of martyrs.

Catherine sits on a throne disputing with some of the scholars gathered together in Alexandria. The miniature is to our knowledge the only representation of this event in which Catherine is enthroned while the Emperor stands; indeed the reverse is normal. Dressed in blue, the one rich color among pale yellows, rose, and green, the saint is the central, dominant person. She looks down in magisterial calm at her adversaries, who when converted will be consigned like their unsuccessful colleagues and their writings to the roaring flames.

A still more interesting departure from tradition is the close and low point of sight. Though the perspective is not systematic the benches boldly overlapped by the lower frame and the decline of the orthogonals create the strong impression that we view the scene from below the frame and look up, even more than do the pagan scholars, to the high throne of the saint.

Fol. 16v St. Catherine cast into Prison.

Then the Emperor [said]: O noble virgin consider well, thou shalt be second only to the Queen and adored by all as a goddess. To him the virgin [replied]: Cease, the very thought is a crime, I have surrendered myself as a bride to Christ, my beloved and my joy.

Maxentius, abandoning hope of shaking Catherine's convictions, supervises her imprisonment. A soldier dressed only in a simple tunic of a beautiful pale yellow—a favorite shade in the *Belles Heures*—raises his cane and uses his knee to propel her forcibly into her cell. The opening is proportionately so small that to enter she must double up. Possibly this arrangement resulted in part from the fact that Paul de Limbourg wanted to maintain his usual large scale for the figures and yet he preferred to show the full height of the building, in the medieval tradition. He himself executed the two principal figures, Jean the others.

Fol. 17 St. Catherine bound to a Column.

Then the King filled with fury ordered her to be given up to scourging, and despatched to a dark prison and tortured there with hunger for twelve days. The Queen, impelled by great desire to visit her, together with the leader of the soldiers came [to her].

The *Golden Legend* tells that Catherine was beaten severely *before* being thrown into prison. Here, however, that episode follows. In Italian painting the scene resembles the Flagellation of Christ. Paul's unique design avoids the whipping entirely and shows her being tied to the column—albeit very forcefully. Each of the soldiers raises a knee to brace himself, a posture that is repeated several times in the manuscript. Catherine exhibits that curious Northern ideal of the female body, best known in Jan van Eyck's *Eve*, that suggests pregnancy or at least fertility as a normal state, though the bodily rotundity surely has no such precise implication here.

Katheuna ugo ānorum. xbuj. pcepto q̃ maxc
cius iptator xanos ad ydolorū facuticet metu
mortis cogeret munita ligno auas au porta
mirabli scie pfunditate ac eloquencie ꝯ fudit.

katuna uirgo .l. mt philosophos et retozes de re
motis ab impatore uocatos argumentoz in zstu
dit et ab ydolorum errorib; reuocas ad xpm ziu
ne quos impator igne succedes mrturio coronau.

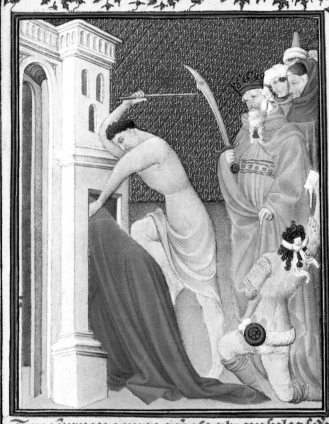

Tunc imperator o uirgo gēnosa tibi consule ꝫ seda
p̃ uirgma reuocabis et a punctis uelut dea adora
beris cu uirgo desine talia q̈ scelus ē cogitare
me xp̄o sponsam tradidi h amorz ꝫ dilecto mea

Tuc rex furoze repletus eā cedi scozpionibz iubet et
obscurum ī carcem mitti ibiq; xij. diebz; fae
cuiaari ad quā uisitandā regina nimio eius
amoze suscensa cum principe militum accedit

Fol. 17v   St. Catherine tended by Angels. PAUL

> *On entering [the Queen] saw in a wondrous light angels anointing the virgin's wounds. After discourse with her on the rewards of eternal life, drawn out until the middle of the night, she converted to the Christian faith.*

Once within the prison, angels salve Catherine's wounds watched by the Empress Faustina who, in the absence of the Emperor, persuades Porphyrius, chief of the guard, to admit her by night. For this intimate scene in the prison, rarely represented, the illuminator has once more chosen a close point of sight, and the entire lower part of the building passes below the frame. The usual blond hues have become even lighter. Catherine's beautiful nude body is surrounded by the pale pink of one angel and the whites of the other two and of her drapery. These tones are perhaps intended to suggest her purity. Together, however, with the elegance and femininity of the figures they compose a group that is unlike anything in earlier Italian or Northern painting. The miniature suggests Renaissance pictures of the toilet of Venus.

Fol. 18   The converted Queen beheaded. PAUL AND JEAN

> *[The Queen] concealed her Christianity until she saw angels destroying the wheels with such force that four thousand pagans were slain. Forthwith she revealed herself and forthwith [Maxentius] ordered her to be beheaded.*

Although the text, following the *Golden Legend*, states that the Queen revealed her conversion only *after* Maxentius had attempted to kill Catherine with spiked wheels, the painter decided to illustrate the two scenes in the reverse order. Since the execution of Porphyrius and his companions follows on folio 19 he doubtless decided to avoid two facing decapitations. The Queen has barely had time to remove her crown as the headsman raises his sword. The composition, which the Limbourgs may have revised, seems less unified than others in this series.

Fol. 18v Angels destroy the Wheel. PAUL

Then the prefect persuaded the furious King to have wheels prepared with iron blades to cut up the virgin. Then the virgin prayed to the Lord to destroy the machine so as to convert the assembled people. Immediately the angels from heaven shattered it.

Since Catherine still persisted in her refusal to worship the pagan gods Maxentius condemned her to the torture that is familiar from her usual attribute. Paul's fearsome wheel, double as in many Trecento paintings, is beautifully carpentered and rich in its texture of wood and metal. The same concern with technique led the painter to depart from iconographic tradition in one notable respect. The text says that the angels of the Lord shattered the instrument of torture. In earlier representations angels appear waving swords but here three of them apply well-constructed claw hammers. Catherine is untouched by the wheels but three men are torn and bleeding. One of them is tossed into a posture that is extraordinary for the art of this time. Doubled up, he lies foreshortened, head foremost—the first of many figures of the kind designed by Paul in this book.

Fol. 19 Beheading of Porphyrius. PAUL AND JEAN

The King, therefore, mad with anger, ordered that the converted Porphyrius and his companions should all be beheaded and the bodies cast to the dogs, and he addressed the virgin saying: Consider well, either thou wilt sacrifice to the gods or I will have thee beheaded.

Porphyrius, captain of the royal guard, secretly buried the Queen's body after her execution. The King, suspecting that it was the work of the executioner, ordered him to be tortured, whereupon Porphyrius admitted his guilt because he, too, had been converted by Catherine. In the contemporary French translation of the *Golden Legend* Maxentius addresses Porphyrius as "guardian of my soul and comfort in all my sorrows." Here the Emperor, desperate at the defection of his favorite, furiously rends his robe.

Paul has again designed figures in unusual and daring positions. The executioner is remarkably powerful. Corpses placed and foreshortened in this way, lacking in Trecento representations of the subject, have a special impact, especially when they spout blood toward the beholder. The King and his companions, much less voluminous, were very probably painted by Jean.

Que cum mirasset uisa mestimabili clarita
te angelos q̄ plagas uirgis iungētes pro tac
toq̄ secum sermone usq̄ ad mediū noctis
de pm̄is esne uite ad xp̄i fidem conuersa est

Celauirqz se xanam donec uidit angelos to
tas cū tanto impetu duellerent qz inj̄ milia
gentiliū moraia ceaderūt unde statim se
manifestat qui eam statim decolari iubet.

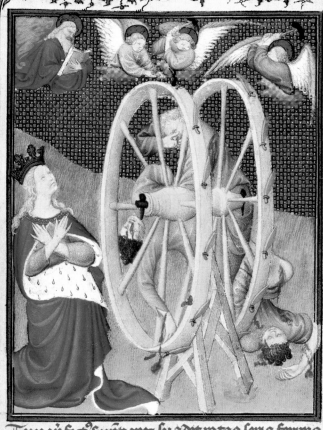

Tunc pfect iuuen regi suadet rotas feris ferreis
jparari ut uirgo delecaretur tunc uirgo dnm dep
catur ut ad conuisione ipli aircunstantis ma
chinā dissiparet z stati angli de cælo ruperunt

Rex autē furore ebrius pstinū cōnsilum et suos
cum milites scpit onis decolari et cozpa canibz
dimitti et ûgine alloquitur diēs aut dijs sac
ficabis bn̄ ꝫ sulta aut te faciam decollari.

Cui katina fac que concepisti tunc decolatta iu
ber que cum ad locu ducta fuist; erectis i celu oclis
orauit dicēs o spes et salus credenciū o deus et
gloria virginū ihū rex bone miserire mei.

Catherine [replied] to him: Do what you have resolved. He ordered that she should be beheaded. Led to the place, raising her eyes to heaven, she prayed saying: O hope and salvation of believers, O honor and glory of virgins, Jesus, perfect king, have mercy upon me.

Since torture had failed to make Catherine recant, the Emperor reluctantly ordered her execution. What fresh observations of the world Paul de Limbourg embodied in his designs is proved by comparison with representations of the same subject by Altichiero or even Masolino. In both the saint's hair remains neatly arranged on her head even at this final moment. Here one lock falls on her breast and the rest of her golden hair hangs straight down between her hands.

The young executioner, looking down at his victim, raises his sword with a vigor as convincing as the peasant with his axe in Paul's small December miniature on folio 13. The rotating figure and the suspended weapon are, in Italian fashion, locked into place by the mountain behind—indeed it provides a kind of counterforce. The sword, stamped with a crown, has a true cutting edge, and Paul has been attentive to such other details as the close-fitting yellow tunic, which is tied back for a freer movement of the figure. The Emperor is entirely resolute whereas an adviser looks at him with a compassionate expression and raises his hand in what might seem to be a remonstrative gesture. The man standing behind, on the other hand, is coarse-featured and impassive. The differentiation of these heads is remarkable, and the painting is no less impressive for the rare beauty of its color.

Angels, however, having received her body, transported it from that place to Mount Sinai, a journey of more than twenty days, and there they buried it. From her bones oil, which heals sickness, flows continuously.

Three angels—one in pale green, another in slate blue, one part white and pink—fly with the body of the saint to the mountainous region of Sinai. Relatively diminutive this landscape may be, but it is unique among paintings of the time. Four utterly barren peaks rise before a vibrant blue sky. One of them is the mountain where Moses received the Law. At the left pilgrims, wearing broad-brimmed hats and equipped like St. James on folio 160v (p. 258) with scrip and staff, move upward through a defile.

Near the center, at the end of the road, there is an exceptionally plain rectangular building. It is built of large gray stones and marked by a couple of string courses. It has a small rectangular addition behind, and a monk or a hermit dressed all in brown (like the Desert Fathers in the Anthony and Paul cycle) sits by the door. No building appears on the mountain in paintings by Altichiero or Masolino, and Paul's structure can only be the monastery of St. Catherine which, built of large stones and surrounded by high walls, looks somewhat like the building in the miniature. French pilgrims constantly visited the monastery; among them were distinguished soldiers such as the Maréchal de Boucicaut and the Duke's son-in-law the Comte d'Eu, for St. Catherine was also a patron of freed prisoners. The French court felt close to the monastery; Charles VI gave it a chalice, and both Jean de Berry and his brother Charles V had stones chipped from the saint's tomb among their collections of relics. The Limbourgs were certainly familiar with descriptions and perhaps a drawing of the monastery. In any event they have given us the earliest depiction of it, and perhaps the first portrait in art of a remote pilgrimage site. They have captured the color, the wild emptiness, and some of the awesome beauty of the mountains. This little miniature clearly foretells the calendar pictures of the *Très Riches Heures.*

Angeli auec corpus eius accipientes ab illo loco
usqz ad monte synay itine plusqz dierum xx
deduxerunt et ibide sepelierut ex au ossibz
Idesi necter olei manat infirmitates sanas.

This is, curiously, the first of the Duke's principal Books of Hours that contain extracts from the Gospels, which normally appear in manuscripts of this kind. Indeed, as John Plummer suggests below, the extracts were not included even when the *Belles Heures* was first planned. In the sequence John, Luke, Matthew, Mark, they began originally with a large miniature of St. John on the island of Patmos. The miniature is now missing but traces of color that have rubbed off onto a blank facing page can be matched with a presumed copy in the Seilern Hours and thus provide us with the lost design.[1]

Whereas John is commonly shown on Patmos, and the lost miniature from the *Belles Heures* is no exception, Matthew does not usually sit on the ground in a landscape. His stern, scowling expression and the strong, saturated colors indicate that Herman painted the miniature.

Matthew is identified by his symbol, the angel. However the rubric, written in alternate lines of blue and red (signs, as we shall see, of a somewhat later execution), makes clear that the text is a passage from Luke. Luke's portrait, in turn, precedes the following extract from Matthew. Possibly the error occurred because the rubrics, like the Psalm titles in the *Très Riches Heures*, were added *after* the paintings had been completed, and the Limbourgs, expecting a different sequence, did not identify the texts. They had no models in the Duke's earlier important Books of Hours but they could have found the symbols of the Evangelists around Christ or the Trinity in Majesty, arranged clockwise from the upper left in a similar sequence.

er inoimus gloriā
eius gloriam quasi
unigeniti a pre ple
nium gracie et uen
tatis. Deo gracias.

Jnicium sancti eu
uangelij secundum
lucam. Gloria tibi
domine qui nar es zc.
N illo tempore.
ecuissus est a

gelus gabriel a deo ī
ciuitatem galilec cui
nomen nazareth t
ad uirginem despon
satam uiro cui nom
erat ioseph de domo
dauid et nomen uir
ginis maria. Et in
gressus angelus ad
eam dixit. Aue ma
ria gracia plena do
minus tecum bene
dicta tu in mulierib.
Q uecum audisset t
turbata est in sermo
ne eius. Et cogitabat
qualis esset ista salu
tacio. Et ait angeluſ
ad eam. Ne timeas
maria inuenisti gra
ciam apud dominū

The rubric for the excerpt from Matthew appears at the bottom of folio 22v and the text itself was written on this folio, but the miniature shows St. Luke with his symbol, the ox.

The Evangelist at work on his Gospel is seated in a high-backed chair placed at an angle before a traceried window, like St. Catherine, the Platonic philosopher in the St. Jerome cycle, or St. Jerome himself (15, 183, 187v). The refined and ornamented building employs a repertoire of motifs that reappear throughout the book: slender columns with beaded capitals, arcaded paneling, a decorated cornice, and acanthus leaves in the spandrels of the arches.

Luke's symbol has the same curving horns as the ox in the *Nativity* (48v, 54v), and it seems to kneel before the saint as it was said to have done at the manger. In color the ox matches the yellow-brown of the vaults and the wood of the chair, while its rose wings blend with the coral tiles and form a transition to the salmon-pink roof of the upper story.

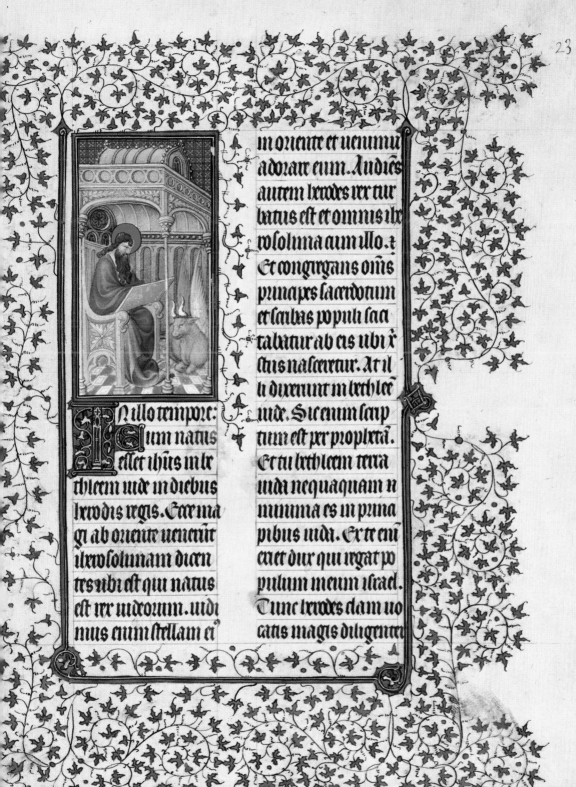

in oriente et uenimus
adorare eum. Audiens
autem herodes rex tur
batus est et omnis ihe
rosolima cum illo. t
Et congregans omis
principes sacerdotum
et scribas populi sci
tabatur ab eis ubi x̄
ctus nasceretur. At il
li dixerunt in bethlee
iude. Sic enim scrip
tum est per prophetā.
Et tu bethleem terra
iuda nequaquam ñ
minima es in princi
pibus iuda. Ex te enī
exiet dux qui regat po
pulum meum israel.
Tunc herodes clam uo
catis magis diligenter

N illo tempore:
Cum natus
esset ihūs in be
thleem iude in diebus
herodis regis. Ecce ma
gi ab oriente uenerunt
iherosolimam dicen
tes ubi est qui natus
est rex iudeorum. uidi
mus enim stellam ei

dium totus mundt orb
terrarum. De te enim
dei filius uerus est om
nipotens deus suam t
sanctissimam fecit n
matrem assumens de
te illam sanctissimam t
carnem per quam mun
dus qui perditus erat
saluatus est. cuius pre
ciosissimo sanguine re

O intemera
ta et met
num be
nedicta singularis at
qz incomparabilis u
go dei genitrix maria
gratissimum dei tem
plum. spus san saca
rium ianua regni ce
lorum per quam post

At the hour of Christ's birth, a very old legend tells, the Tiburtine Sibyl led the Emperor Augustus to the place on the Campidoglio in Rome now occupied by the Church of Araceli, and there pointed out to him, in the sky, the Virgin and Child surrounded by a golden radiance. This vision began to be represented in France in the late fourteenth century, and Jean de Berry became its chief sponsor. He introduced it into his Books of Hours, beginning with the one now in Brussels, and in the *Belles Heures* it provides a novel illustration for one of the two common prayers to the Virgin. Its connection with this prayer—*O Intemerata*—confirms our thought that the Duke favored the subject because he liked to associate himself with the Emperor Augustus, for the illustration of the prayer often showed the donor, not the Emperor, kneeling before the Virgin.

In this, their first representation of the subject, the Limbourgs—or rather Jean who probably painted the Madonna while Herman executed the two figures below—confused it with another subject, derived from the twelfth chapter of Revelation, the purity of the Virgin. The Virgin does not appear, as she should, in the sun but on a sickle moon; the moon, however, is golden. The Limbourgs corrected their iconographic mistake in the *Très Riches Heures*, whereas their error with the Evangelists was, oddly, repeated in the later manuscript.

This miniature begins the cycle of the Hours of the Virgin. The Angel Gabriel, his wings moving and his mantle stirred, enters the Virgin's chamber through the open arch and falls on one knee to announce the incarnation. As the celestial messenger he often carries a scroll or a staff; here, however, he holds the large lilies that are usually placed in a vase beside Mary as a symbol of her perpetual virginity. He looks up and points to the dove descending in a shower of golden rays. The kneeling Virgin turns as she does in a miniature by Jacquemart in the Duke's *Brussels Hours,* a book that the Limbourgs certainly knew. Here, however, she does not look at Gabriel but casts her eyes down humbly. With equal humility she crosses her hands on her breast, as in Italian representations; from them derive also the stars on her mantle.

The Duke's *Meditations* preserves the tradition that when the angel appeared the Virgin had been reading a Messianic prophecy from Isaiah: "Behold a virgin shall conceive and bear a son . . ." Here she kneels before a lectern with an inscribed scroll that perhaps represents that text. According to the apocryphal gospel of Pseudo-Matthew the Virgin was "the best informed in the law of God . . ." In the miniature her lectern is appropriately surmounted by a statue of Moses holding the tablets of the Law. A book lies open on the lectern, and there are two more volumes below. Earlier French representations of the Annunciation contain a single book; the open hutch containing books beneath the lectern appeared earlier only in the Hannover altarpiece by Meister Bertram of Hamburg.

God the Father occupies a projecting balcony supported by a caryatid who may represent a prophet. Although he is a comparatively small figure his color, gray-violet, influences the design, reappearing in the ceiling, the shadows in Gabriel's mantle, and the tiles of the floor.

In the exceptionally rich and strong border Paul repeated the Virgin's blue. The acanthus arabesque on a broad band, unprecedented in French illumination, was suggested by the work of an Italian illuminator of the Duke, the Brussels Initials Master, but Paul probably took some of the specific forms from the Porta della Mandorla of the Cathedral of Florence. In addition to angels, prophets, and the arms of the Duke the borders contain his emblems: swans, bears, and, probably in the same category, snails.

ommela ——— rabit laudem tuam
bia mea ———— eus in adiuto
apues ——— rium meum
Etos meum dni ——— intende

Deus in ad
iutorium
meum
intende.

Domine ad adiu
uandum me festina.
Gloria patri et filio
et spiritui sancto.

After his salutation to the Virgin the Angel Gabriel told her that her aged cousin Elizabeth had miraculously conceived a son and that she was already in the sixth month of her pregnancy. "And Mary arose in those days, and went into the hill country with haste, into a city of Juda" (Luke 1: 39). Pilgrims to the Holy Land described the site of their meeting as a spring of fresh water near a ruined castle said to be Zachariah's house, situated in a valley just off the road that led from Bethlehem to Jerusalem.

Paul, who probably designed and partly painted the miniature, placed the figures near a high, arched entrance gate. The Virgin is a grave and graceful young woman clasping her rose-covered book, whereas the aging Elizabeth has strong and homely features. The painter has heightened the contrast between the two women by differentiating their haloes, giving the Virgin solid gold and Elizabeth golden rays. Elizabeth bends forward with outstretched hand, saying "Blessed art thou among women and blessed is the fruit of thy womb . . . For, lo, as soon as the voice of thy salutation sounded in mine ears, the babe leaped in my womb for joy" (Luke 1: 42, 44).

The two figures are held closely together by the green peak that rises sharply behind, isolating them from the bare hills crowned by two walled towns that perhaps represent Bethlehem and Jerusalem. The Virgin closely resembles St. Catherine on 15v. Although she seems less voluminous and more ornamental, and thus more related to Jean, the painting of her tunic is extraordinary. The green glistens with a golden yellow where it catches the light, and it is shot with a rose that reflects the color of Elizabeth's dress.

eus in ad   omine ad adiu
iutorium   uandum me festina
meum in   loria pri et filio z
tende.   spiritui sancto.

Christ is born in a humble shelter, used in bad weather, according to the Duke's French version of the *Meditations,* to tether beasts of burden in the market place. The thatched roof, which began to show conspicuous holes in paintings of this period, is here exceptionally dilapidated. Through the exposed rafters the rays of the miraculous star shine on the Virgin and her Child. Mary, lacking a bed, sits humbly on the ground beside the manger.

After the birth of the Child, according to the Duke's *Meditations,* Joseph sat "quite dejected because he was unable to provide the Virgin Mary with everything necessary." The text also says that, as a carpenter, he did what he could to enclose the place for her protection. Here he rests his head pensively on his hand after having made a small fire to heat a pot and to check the chill of December.

Usually the Virgin is provided with at least a cushion or pad but she lacks even this simple comfort already in Sienese fourteenth-century panels. This type of humble Virgin was copied in the kind of Florentine embroidery that the Duke of Berry possessed in great numbers, and which thus transmitted Trecento figures and compositions to his painters. In the Italian models a kneeling shepherd is present. Here two shepherds, smaller than the sacred figures, already adore the newborn Child, although the angel only gives them the good tidings in the miniature for Terce that follows. The *Meditations* says that, to express their joy, they brought with them rural musical instruments, including a bagpipe. The shepherd who carries it here seems transfixed by the great star in the sky. The ox also looks up at it while the ass gazes at the Child.

The figures participate to an extraordinary degree in a broad geometric design, unprecedented in Northern painting and a clear consequence of Paul's comprehension of Trecento Florentine art. Un-Florentine, however, are the wide spatial intervals within the composition. The strongest movement in the scene, the shepherd's gesture, is locked into the geometric pattern. From it the two conical mountains ascend and diverge, creating a strong centripetal counterforce.

"And, lo, the angel of the Lord came upon them, and the glory of the Lord shone round about them: and they were sore afraid" (Luke 2:9).

The Annunciation to the Shepherds was commonly represented as a separate scene only in the fourteenth century, and it then assumed a place in French Books of Hours. The scene gave the prominence to simple people that the Adoration of the Magi had given to nobility. According to the Duke's version of the *Meditations* the shepherds looked up to see three suns that afterwards merged into one, and here the two herdsmen shade their eyes to watch three angels with golden haloes announcing the birth of the Messiah and singing the *Gloria* from their open book. The angels, resting on a puffy mass of blue clouds, are linked to each other, to the violet book, and to the shepherds in a beautiful interchange of color. Green draperies and rose wings alternate with green wings and a rose cloak that is echoed in the rose hood of the shepherd below, dressed in the same buff as the center angel. The second shepherd wears a rough tunic of skin with a cape that seems to be made from the wool of the flock that peacefully huddles beneath the trees or crops the green pasture. The hungry goat stretching to reach a higher branch in a tree has a long history in art, but the animal scratching his head with a hind leg is a lively detail added by the painter from fresh observation of nature. A long lean whippet with a red collar, reclining but with ears pricked, looks as if he has wandered in from the aristocratic world to serve as a watch dog.

As usual Paul, following Florentine precedent, took care to maintain a balance at both sides of a central axis. It is marked here by the middle angel; slightly to the left lies the hat whereas the shepherds stand at the right. Toward the left, however, the city of Jerusalem appears at the horizon and, nearer the frame, there is a golden hill illuminated from above and crowned by the towers of Bethlehem. The rendering of the distant buildings in pale blue reflects the growing attention by the Limbourgs to aerial perspective.

Deus in ad
iutorium
meum t
intende.

Domine ad adiu
uandum me festia.
Gloria pri et filio
et spiritui sancto.

The Three Kings, led by the star to the Christ Child, kneel to present their gifts. Matthew refers to them laconically as "wise men from the East" but already in the early centuries of the Church they were spoken of as kings and their number was fixed at three, perhaps because of their triple offering of gold, frankincense and myrrh. Under their traditional names, Melchior, Gaspar, and Balthasar, they came to represent not only the homage of the Gentile world to Christ but the three ages of man. Melchior, old and gray-bearded, presents his gold, Gaspar, a mature man with dark hair and beard, brings frankincense, and Balthasar, young, fair-haired and beardless, offers myrrh.

Melchior has as usual laid aside his crown, but Gaspar and Balthasar are also doffing theirs—a gesture for which the only precedent appears to be a somewhat earlier diptych, probably of Netherlandish origin, now in the Bargello in Florence. There, too, as in Italian paintings, horses from the royal train appear in the background, although none quite like the gray charger throwing back his head, to neigh perhaps, in recognition of the miraculous star. Nearby a shepherd kneels in adoration.

The Virgin in her humble shelter was seated on the ground in Paul's miniature for the *Nativity* (fol. 48v), but now the painter has provided her with a bed covered in royal scarlet. A massive figure, larger in scale than the others, she holds on her lap the sturdy curly-headed Child, naked except for the mantle she has tucked about his legs. Joseph, the carpenter, kneels facing Melchior. The two men are similar in age and mien, but the King is dressed in rose and saffron decorated with gold whereas Joseph wears a subdued brown and violet mantle, beautifully set off by a mustard-yellow tunic. His head is covered only by a white skull cap; his pointed hat, like the crowns of the Kings, has been removed. On the hill by the road leading down from Jerusalem a golden statue of Mars stands on a column, representing the pagan world and the military domination of Rome.

Forty days after the Nativity the Holy Family came to Jerusalem so that Mary might be purified in accordance with the Law and the Child presented in the Temple. The violet altar is placed in an unusual triangular structure open to somber green hills. Following the precedent of Jacquemart in the Duke's *Brussels Hours* Paul has wished to give the building great scale; one broad arch spans three figures and a wall rises beyond the frame, apparently to a great height. The figures themselves are monumental. Paul has represented only the main protagonists: the Virgin holding her child above the altar, Simeon "the just and devout" to whom it had been revealed "that he should not see death before he had seen the Lord's Christ" (Luke 2:25, 26), and the aged prophetess Anna, who holds a long beeswax candle. Other figures who usually appear—Joseph, a female attendant with the sacrificial doves, and the High Priest—are not included.

Simeon, his hands covered by the white and gold cloth, prepares to take the Child from his mother. In doing so he parts the legs in a manner that suggests the related scene of the circumcision. Jesus, the same robust child we have seen in the *Nativity* and *Adoration,* seems reluctant to go to the old man and clings to his mother's neck. Simeon hails Christ as "a light to lighten the Gentiles" and the taper held by the devout old Anna is a reminder that candles are blessed and carried in procession as part of the ritual of the feast of February 2nd, popularly known as Candlemas.

A scroll in the border bears the first verses of the Penitential Psalm 51: "Misere mei Deus secundum magnam misericordiam tuam Et secundum multitudinem miserationum tuarum dele iniquitatem meam Amplius lava me domine ab iniqui[tate]. . . ." ("Have mercy upon me, O God, according to thy loving kindness: according unto the multitude of thy tender mercies blot out my transgressions. Wash me thoroughly from my sin. . . .") The quotation would seem more appropriate to the purification ceremony of any woman other than the Virgin for, as the Duke's version of the *Meditations* is careful to stress, she was and remained a virgin. She conformed to the Law, however, to indicate that Jesus had come to fulfill and not to destroy it.

This miniature differs in style from the preceding ones by Paul in the Hours of the Virgin, and it was probably painted somewhat later. The surfaces are more luminous, and the draperies show more lively curvatures than in any other of Paul's paintings. Anna and Simeon are also unusually attenuated. This is surely Paul's work, however. The color alone proves that, ranging as it does from a soft tan, mustard, violet and rose to a subtly graded white and a superb clear blue.

eus mad   Domine ad adiu
utronū   uandum me festia
meum   Gloria pri et filio
intende.   et spirituy sancto

Eusm   Domineadadumá
adiuto   dum me festina.
num me   Gtoria pri et filio et
rum intende spiritui sancto.

The subject, unusual in French Books of Hours, did appear a century earlier in manuscripts illuminated by Jean Pucelle and his circle. He introduced it for None in the *Hours of Jeanne de Savoie*, painted about 1320, and as a bas-de-page at Sext in the *Hours of Jeanne d'Evreux*, which then belonged to Jean de Berry and is now in the Cloisters. It was used again at None in the Duke's own *Très Belles Heures de Notre Dame*. In Pucelle's miniatures Herod, with crossed legs, presides over the slaughter. In the *Belles Heures*, however, the painter has presented the subject as two consecutive scenes.

Enthroned in his palace Herod, infuriated that the Magi have departed without giving him news of the Christ Child, hands to a kneeling soldier the order for a mass murder of all boys born in the district of Bethlehem over the previous two years. An adviser stands behind the throne.

The massacre takes place against a landscape dominated by the walled city of Jerusalem on the horizon. A rather vapid mother in blue has had her child snatched by a soldier who dangles him by the legs. More animated is the guard raising his scimitar to dismember a baby suspended above his knee.

The Mass for the Feast of the Innocents associates the victims with St. John's vision of Revelation 14: 1: ". . . lo, a Lamb stood on the mount Sion, and with him an hundred forty and four thousand, having his Father's name written in their foreheads." Not surprisingly, therefore, relics of the infant martyrs were particularly numerous. Ogier d'Anglure, a contemporary pilgrim, was shown a great cofferful when he passed through Venice, so it cannot have been difficult for the Doge to provide the Duke with one entire Innocent and a leg complete with foot. In addition his inventories list a pair of legs joined at the waist, which we see here among the dismembered limbs.

Warned by Joseph's dream that Herod was preparing to kill the Christ Child the Holy Family fled to Egypt. Paul sought to make of this episode, as of the *Purification*, a monumental composition. He wished to emulate the Italian panel and mural painters, and the work of Giotto and his followers served him not only as sources of style but of specific forms, such as the flying angel, the rocky peak, and the ridge descending from it toward St. Joseph, who looks backward.

Despite Paul's admiration for the fresco of the Flight in the Arena Chapel, which he might recently have seen, he probably judged it to be rather static and abstract. He was seeking greater movement and luminosity, not to mention varied texture and in general a more intimate view of the world. No one before him had described the prints of hoofs and feet in the dust of the road. Herman repeated these observations on 72 (p. 256), and then Paul himself transferred the prints to snow in his superb *February* in the *Très Riches Heures*.

Of course such innovations reflect sensibilities cultivated in the North, and Paul could take advantage even of a Northern posture to accomplish in the end what we may characterize as an Italian effect. The averted Virgin had been introduced only in 1393 into the French and Flemish representations of the Flight, and Paul adopted the figure to bring mother and son close together while giving a special prominence to the child. It suggested to him also—and this is his most genial development of the posture —the possibility of a corresponding rotation of Joseph. The two turning figures are so powerful in their interrelated movement that they bring to mind later contraposto in the work of Donatello or Quercia.

Alongside Paul's forceful Virgin and Joseph the ass appears especially quiet and meek. His soft hair is lighted, it seems, chiefly by reflection from the road. The Virgin is a broad, heavy figure, and Paul, feeling she needed more support than the little gray ass could give her, extended her mantle below it to serve as a vertical buttress.

In largeness of conception and control of color this imposing miniature approximates the later miniatures in the manuscript, including those near the end. Like the Baptism on 211v the *Flight* has a masterful simplicity and a similar harmony of tan, gold, pale green, violet, and blue.

onuerte
nos deus
salutaris
noster:

Et auerte iram tu
am a nobis.
Deus in adiuto
rium meum

Fol. 66   David's Enemies destroyed. *Psalm 6.*

The seven Penitential Psalms usually form part of a Book of Hours but rarely is each one of them illustrated. Even the Duke's well-known Psalter would not have provided the Limbourgs with models because it contains only the usual miniatures marking the eight principal divisions of the book. For a few miniatures in the *Belles Heures* the Vulgate titles suggested the subject, and for others the painters or their advisers chose a verse of the psalm or an interpretation for which we have found no precedent.

The first psalm of this penitential exercise is enriched by a broad gold frame. For King David the painter provided a royal background of fleurs-de-lys. In answer to his prayer "Let all my enemies be ashamed and sore vexed" a pirouetting angel with a fiery red cloak drives a spear through the last of his adversaries. The vanquished lie bleeding as they have fallen pell-mell. The restless pattern as well as the combination of blue-green, vermillion, cool blue, and ruddy flesh imply the authorship of Herman.

Fol. 71v   David calls on the Lord. *Psalm 130.*

"Out of the depths have I cried unto thee, O Lord. Lord hear my voice." To illustrate the opening words of the psalm the painter has chosen to show the young David with a companion, hiding in a cave from the wrath of King Saul. Behind a curved wattle fence sits a burly man in blue with a cloth cap pulled down over his eyes. Holding a large key, he has fallen asleep, his back turned to the cave, so that he looks like an incompetent jailer. David, his hands crossed prayerfully, looks up to the Deity in anxious expectation: "I wait for the Lord, my soul doth wait, and in his word do I hope."

Et anima mea t
turbata est valde sed tu
domine usquequo
Convertere domine
et eripe animam meam
saluum me fac prop
ter misericordiam tuam.
Quoniam non e
in morte qui memor
sit tui in inferno autem
quis confitebitur tibi.
Laboraui in gemi
tu meo lauabo per sin
gulas noctes lectum
meum lacrimis meis
stratum meum rigabo.
Turbatus est a furo
re oculus meus inuet
aui inter omnes ini
micos meos.
Discedite a me omis

Domine ne
in furore
tuo argu
as me neque in ira tua
corripias me.
Miserere mei domine
quoniam infirmus
sum sana me domine
quoniam conturbata
sunt ossa mea

naao eſt et propter lege
tiam ſuſtinui te dne.

Suſtinuit anima
mea in uerbo eius ſpe
rauit anima mea in
domino

Acustodia matuti
na uſq; ad noctem ſpe
ret iſrael in domino.

Quia apud dnm
miſericordia et copio
ſa apud eum redemp
tio

Et ipſe redimet iſr̄l̄
ex omnibus iniquita
tibus eius.

Gloria pr̄i et filio z
ſpiritui ſancto.

Siait erat in prina
pio et nunc et ſemper z
in ſecula ſeculorum.

De profundis
clamaui ad
te domine: domine er
audi uocem meam.

Fiant aures tue i
tendentes in uocem de
precationis mee.

Si iniquitates ob
ſeruaueris domine tr
domine quis ſuſtineb.

Quia apud te propi

In the time of Pope Gregory the Great the litanies were instituted. Whereas the Romans lived temperately during Lent and after that relaxed all restraints, God, provoked, sent them the bubonic plague. Wherefore Gregory instituted the litanies.

The second special cycle is not only, like the first, novel in a Book of Hours but for the most part novel in the history of art. The first three miniatures tell the story of the event that, according to the *Golden Legend*, occurred in 590. Pope Gregory, wearing the triple tiara, addresses a throng in words inspired by the Holy Ghost. Numerous men seated on the ground respond by lifting their eyes to heaven. At the foot of the pulpit two cardinals sit quite unmoved, reading their books. In the foreground one man with pallid face, wearing a tattered tunic, falls to the ground with his mouth open as if sneezing, a symptom of the plague described by the text on the following page. The acolytes bearing the cross and the standards hold their ground but two bystanders flee in terror.

The four miniatures of this cycle contain rare colors in unusual combinations. The blue of the inscriptions is repeated in the fields of the miniatures. To it Paul added scarlet, pink, chocolate, and violet, with violet lying in the shadows on scarlet. With these stronger colors he mixed white, buff, lemon, saffron, and pale green. Nothing fresher and more beautiful can be seen in all of fifteenth-century painting.

Fol. 73v   The Great Litany Procession.   PAUL

It is said that the plague was so violent that people, suddenly sneezing in the road, at table, at the games, died. Whenever one heard someone sneezing there was hardly time to aid him with "God help you" before he expired.

Pope Gregory, now wearing only a bishop's miter and without his halo, raises his hands in supplication. He is followed by the cardinals, a friar, laymen and perhaps a woman, who pour out of the Flaminian Gate, representing, as the *Golden Legend* tells us, the seven categories of persons who took part in the original procession. Chanting clerics have joined the acolytes bearing standards, but the mortality still continues. Two of the Limbourg brothers, Jean and Herman, had witnessed such scenes before they fled from Paris during an outbreak of plague from 1399 to 1402.

The scampering man in yellow with a violet peaked hat may be an actor or jester who has come from the "games" mentioned in the title. He begins to bless the man who has already died. We seem to see from a different angle the same prostrate man in blue who appeared in the preceding miniature. He lies foreshortened, his head toward the picture plane, like the prone figures in the Catherine cycle (18v, 19). Paul was intensely interested in such experiments in dramatic perspective, and the Litany is remarkable for innovations in form, as exciting and sensitive as those in color.

Fol. 74   End of the Plague.

At last after a great carnage of people, mourning, fasts, weighty penances, while the Pope was going through Rome with the entire populace and clergy, an angel appeared on the great palace sheathing his drawn, blood-stained sword.

The plague ended when St. Michael sheathed his sword over Hadrian's monument, from then on known as Castel Sant'Angelo. Although Paul's building does not closely resemble the Castello, it has a similar imposing scale, achieved by extending the miniature into the area of the border.

In other approximately contemporary representations of this event the procession reaches the castle as the archangel appears. Paul, however, followed the title, omitting the procession and concentrating on the carnage.

A corpse is lowered into a freshly dug grave, strikingly brown against the light greensward. Two powerful men hold another large corpse even more daring in position than comparable figures in the preceding miniatures. Only the damned in certain scenes of the Last Judgment would have shown Paul similar figures. Perhaps this is another hint that he had seen Giotto's frescoes in Padua.

Fol. 74v   Procession of Flagellants.

And this custom is observed until the present day: men go nude in some places, beating themselves and tormenting the flesh in fasting and prayer and lamentation, invoking the protection of all the saints in procession.

This miniature illustrates the last day of one of the annual Lesser Litany or Rogation processions. According to the *Golden Legend* it was customary, particularly in France, to carry a stuffed dragon representing the devil. On the first two days it preceded the cross to symbolize the era of the Old Dispensation. On the last day, as a sign that Christ had defeated the devil, the cross headed the procession.

The title is not, however, drawn from the *Golden Legend*, which does not mention flagellation. This form of self-mortification was practiced by thousands after each outbreak of the plague. In Italy flagellants, like three in Paul's miniature, were normally garbed in white with openings only for their eyes and on their shoulders. In the North, however, as here, they sometimes wear dark hats and are bare to the waist.[2]

In Paul's miniature two men fall to the ground, apparently for a more vigorous whipping. The painter masterfully combines their fixed postures with the movement of the group by extending their arms to create a forward flow. The color of the miniature is as beautiful as it is exceptional, all white and flesh, except for the pale yellow-green grass and the brown of the hats and the hair—a simple yet subtle pattern that anticipates, if one dares say it, Piero della Francesca. The touches of bright blood on the backs of the flagellants serve to maintain the relationship with the red of the title below, though on this folio it is the white of the vellum, the blue of the script, and the gold of the ivy that reappear most prominently in the miniature and its background.

Tempore magni gregouj pp. mstitute fuerunt
letanie qz cū romani ī. xlª. conuncter uurisset et p̄
ca luxurie frena laxarent puocatus dn̄s in eos
pestem mguinariā mısit ūc letanias gr̄ istitui.

Tam leua aut illa peſtis fuiſſe fertur q̃ boïes ĩ ma ĩ
menſa inludis ſubito ſternutando morerẽtur
vnde cum aliquis ſternutante audiebat uix ieͥ
auxilium diͨbat adiuuerᵗᵉ te dſ et ſpm eralabat.

Tandē p' stragem hoīm maximā luct' icunia et
pīnas graues ī̄p processionalr eunti p̄ romā cū
inuisa plebe et clero apparet angelus sanguino
lentū enšē imagina reponens sup palaciū magī

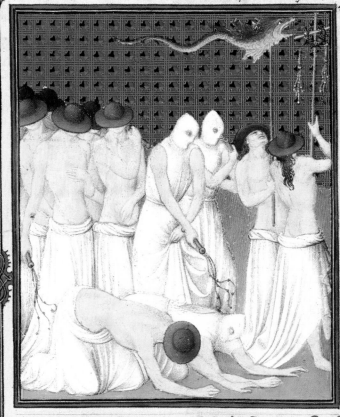

Seruatur q̈ hec confuetudo ulq̈ i hodiernū diē
q̈ homines uadūt nudi maliquibꝫ locis iuera
tes se et macerando carnē iu ieiunio et oꝛone et
planctu pꝛeffionalr oīm sc̄oꝛ pꝛocinia iploꝛāte

omine la cabit laudem tuam.
bia mea a eus madinto
pnes. & riu men itede.
tos menm annii Domine ad adinuā

Fol. 80 Descent from the Cross.

The Friday Office of the Hours of the Cross is usually introduced by a miniature of the Crucifixion. Perhaps because the Hours of the Passion in the *Belles Heures* includes no less than three scenes of Christ on the cross, Paul, who surely designed and at least partially painted this miniature, chose for it an exceptional theme. The action of lowering the body from the cross has been halted. Christ is mourned by his companions and his body is displayed to the beholder. The composition is thus a precursor of the famous *Lamentation* by Roger van der Weyden in the Prado. Paul replaced realistic accessories such as ladders with the slender converging diagonals of the lance and reed. They provide a fiction of support to the two symmetrical angels, who though quite substantial lack lower limbs and end in floating draperies. The corpse is not easily held upright, although the figures press against it as buttresses. The man at the right (Nicodemus?) beneath Christ's arm tries hard, but Joseph of Arimathea remains rather detached. Perhaps that is why in the end the painter, confused about his role, made him an oddly mannered figure. The two angels are related in color to figures diagonally opposite in the compact principal group. The four grieving angels in the quatrefoils of the richly decorated frame are also arranged diagonally in pairs, two with blue tunics on red backgrounds and two in pink on blue. Similarly two pray and two lament.

Fol. 84 Pentecost. *Hours of the Holy Ghost.*

The painter has given the house where the disciples assembled an ecclesiastical form, and the structure behind the Virgin is an apse. This is probably the first miniature in the book in which the projection above, here circular, was originally planned. To dramatize the descent of the Spirit Paul wanted a high building, the scale of which seems increased by the lowliness of the figures; kneeling or sitting, they look up to the radiance below the vaults. Although the figures are confined to the lower space they seem, as so often in the painter's work, more robust than the building. Indeed the contrast increases the size of the remarkably voluminous Virgin, who sits quietly, arms crossed humbly, in a very narrow space. The apostle at the left has a truly Giottesque stature, and his color, rose on mustard—a combination favored by Paul—recalls Altichiero. The apostles, numbering sixteen rather than the usual twelve, are individualized with respect to both physiognomy and expression, but the tripartite design, the symmetrical groups of apostles, and the tranquil frontality of the Virgin join to create a very formal scene. The color, too, is balanced not only laterally but vertically, particularly by the introduction above of red bricks and a strip of blue sky.

Once again Paul's touches of color—mustard and pink-violet on gray-green, rose on pale yellow-green—seem absolutely magical.

ominne la   aabit laudem tuam.

bia mea   eus madututo

aperies.   uum meum

tos meum annū   intende.

The portrait of the Duke appears opposite the prayer for the Assumption. He kneels in the sort of private oratory we know he had in the choir of the Sainte-Chapelle in Bourges and no doubt also in his other chapels. Although the context of the miniature is religious, the portrait is given political allusions by the coronet and by the mace and the arm of a partially visible attendant.

Pentimenti clearly show, even in the color plate, that the Duke originally had another object on his head, possibly a turban of the kind worn on secular occasions by other nobles of the time but not known in any of the numerous surviving portraits of Jean de Berry. Only in one portrait of him at prayer, a later miniature in Bourges, does he wear a hat on his head. In other comparable miniatures he is either bareheaded or wearing a coronet, so that he or his counselors may have objected to the original turban.

Infrared light discloses that the Duke was not at first envisaged in exact profile, but turned slightly toward us, so that the far eye was visible, the collar and mantle broader, and one hand, at least, extended farther. There seem to be traces of a necklace and pendant, never elsewhere put on over his state robe with ermine collar. These indications, together with the clear signs of a turban, suggest a more informal portrait than we now see.

Under the blue robe the Duke is dressed in an exceptional manner: a tight green tunic and red hose. Most puzzling of all is his youth. In other portraits between ca. 1406 and 1409 he wears a small goatee or beard. The clean-shaven face here suggests a date about 1405, when the Duke was around sixty-five years old. The discrepancy in age is so great we might begin to suspect another sitter, but although the drapery over the prie-dieu displays simply the fleur-de-lys, without any special emblem of Berry, the evidence in the manuscript for the presence of the Duke is compelling. His youthful appearance, which surpasses the usual limits of idealization and of flattery, was perhaps inspired by a wish to reduce the contrast between a man of sixty-five and his twenty-eight year old second wife.

Puzzling, too, are the discrepancies in scale between the Duke and the macebearer, who is much too large for his position in the composition as indicated by his feet on the tiled floor. Similarly the curtain, hanging from a rod apparently in the foreground, seems to be pulled back deep in the space. These uncertainties point to Jean rather than to Paul as the designer of the miniature.

enlumine mon auer et de leur uies amen
a lui seruir et amer. der. Aue maria gra.

A ue maria gra a a.

Oracio. xb. ad bam
mariam p gaudiu qd
huit i die assupcois sue.

T res doulce da
me pour prel
le grant ioie que no°
eustes au iour de uie
assumpaon quant
ure cher filz uous por
ta es aelx et uous co
ronna sur toutes fe
mes du monde. dou
ce pries li pour moy
et pour tous pecheurs
et toutes pecherelles
que par sa digne puis
sance ilz aient uolete
dsir hors de leur pechie

quant nous enuoia
stes nir saint angle
gabriel a la uierge ma
rie dire et annuncier la
nouuelle et le conseil
de nir loy biau sire dien
si comme ce fu uoir no
uueilues regarder en
pitie et nous donner nie
sainte miseucorde. Am.

Pater nir qui es i cielis.

oulr dieu
doulx pere
sainte tri
nitte .j. dieu biau sur
dieu ie uous requier
conseil et aide en lon
neur et a la rimembra
ce de celuy hautisime co
seil que uous prenstes
de nir ppre sapience est

f. 91 v°

Fol. 91v   The Duchess praying to the Trinity.

This portrait, on the verso of the Duke's, must be his Duchess. It is the first and only instance of a representation of either of Jean de Berry's two wives in a manuscript. When he married Jeanne de Boulogne in 1389 he was forty-nine and she was only twelve, so that her youthful appearance here, unlike his, presents no problem. On their marriage contract the Duchess is shown wearing a dress of the same cut as her blue gown in the miniature. A long floating veil hangs from her head and, like Salome's on folio 212v, it is caught up on the hip. She wears a royal crown, unsuitable to a duchess. Although there are no clear signs of alteration could it conceivably have been added when Yolande, the Duchess of Anjou, who was also Queen of Sicily, acquired the manuscript soon after the death of Jean de Berry? Despite the prie-dieu and the curtains, which indicate an interior, the ground is green and there is a blue sky.

The text is a prayer to God the Father, "Holy Trinity, one God," invoking his mercy in the name of the Annunciation. The prayer might have had a personal connotation. All the sons of Jean de Berry were dead by this time and Jeanne de Boulogne had remained childless. The prayer could thus contain a hope.

The Trinity is represented in a form quite new to the Duke's Books of Hours. Instead of the two persons in human form with the Holy Ghost as a dove spreading his wings between them, or (another type) God holding the crucified Christ and a dove flying between them, the three figures are all identical, old and bearded. Father, Son and Holy Ghost are dressed alike, and they wear the triple tiara usually reserved for God the Father alone. When devising this representation the Limbourgs may have been influenced by a miniature in the Duke's *Petites Heures* which shows God approaching Abraham in the form of three identical men.

The Trinity is surrounded by a luminous yellow disk that resembles a golden halo. The deep blue sky grows brighter beneath the semicircle of cherubim and the green horizon dips down toward the kneeling Duchess. The cooler and darker colors in her space, conspicuously violet and deep blue, are subtly blended with varying shades of rose.

Fol. 94   Diocrès expounding the Scriptures.

In about the year 1084 a certain well-known man, famous and professor of Holy Writ, reached the end of his days. Clerics and others assembled in Paris to celebrate his obsequies with accustomed honors.

The third cycle of miniatures is the first known representation of the story of an eminent theologian of the eleventh century, Raymond Diocrès, and of the foundation of the Carthusian Order by St. Bruno, who had been deeply impressed by the strange events that followed his death. The titles in this cycle, which follow the first life of Bruno written in the thirteenth century, refer to Diocrès simply as a well-known scholar and to Bruno as "Master" Bruno. Since the founder of the Carthusians was not canonized he appears in the *Belles Heures* without a halo. No earlier representations of Diocrès are extant and of Bruno we have found only four single scenes; there are, however, unverifiable reports of stories from his life painted in the fourteenth-century Charterhouse in Paris.

Diocrès faces us in an imposing raised *cathedra*. Scholars, monks, and clerics in their academic gowns, among them perhaps Bruno in blue, have gathered around him for discussion and transcription. So buried is he in his work that only the top of his head rises above the large lectern—a very bold perspective device at this period. Although his face is hidden the rapidly flowing folds of his mantle assure us of his intellectual vigor. The great informality implied by his posture is maintained by the casual asymmetry of the disciples. The impressive recession of planes all parallel to the picture plane was no doubt designed by Paul de Limbourg, and the neatly morticed joints of the bench in the foreground as well as the threaded shaft of the revolving bookstand are typical of his interest in practical detail. The execution of the miniature does not, however, seem to be his.

Circa annos domini. cƆ.lxxxuiƒ. uir quidã ma
gni nois atq; fame sacre pagine. pfessor. ad extre
mũ uite pductus ẽ. vnde tã clerici qm alij ad ei'
exequias honorifice ut mon̄ ẽ pti' co̅uenerũt

Fol. 94v   Diocrès cries out.

But when the corpse of the deceased was about to be placed in the grave, surrounded by all the bystanders, it called out saying: I have been justly accused in the judgment of God. Hearing this all those present, dumbfounded, carried the corpse into the church to await the morrow.

The miniature does not represent the scene described by the title but a similar episode on the following day to which the text on the facing page refers. For this amazing event the painter chose a diagonal design and a fast recession in the church, with its floor of violet and olive-green tiles and its deep blue vaults visible in the distance. The beholder, though nearby, is held at a distance from the miraculous event by an entrance arch.

The rich cloth, black over tan, slips off the coffin as Diocrès raises the lid and opens his mouth to cry out, the words moving into space like the uninscribed scroll that emerges from his hand. The friars who have gathered in the choir to recite the Office of the Dead show their astonishment by twisting and turning, each gesturing in a different way.

Fol. 95   The Burial of Diocrès.   PAUL

The following day, while the obsequies were being celebrated, the defunct again cried out: I have been justly accused in the judgment of God. Then [the bystanders], greatly astonished, deliberated because the judgment could be for good or for evil and reserved [the decision] awaiting the next day.

On the next day, as the coffin is lowered into the freshly dug grave, the lid again opens and the corpse announces that he is damned. Ignoring this assertion the friars continue to chant and a thurifer sprinkles holy water. The ceremonial mourners remain imperturbable, except one who leans forward in amazement at the open coffin. The man in pink who raises a hand to bless perhaps represents Bruno.

Paul de Limbourg, who painted this miniature, enjoyed as usual the description of the coffin, the ropes and the postures of the men working them, the tools used to dig, and the exhumed bones of a predecessor.

The two processions converging on the grave compose a triangle reaching deep into space, and the ceremonial mourners form a vertical extending back from its apex near the picture plane. The geometric pattern is clothed, so to speak, in beautiful colors, most of them light and set off by the fine dark gray of the ceremonial mourners as well as by the brown of the earth—freshly excavated and as amorphous as smoke. The marvelously delicate tans, pinks, and greens shaded in violet are echoed in the distance. There, on the light greensward of the cemetery, the varicolored tombslabs are scattered like spring flowers.

On the morrow, all being assembled for the burial of the deceased, again the corpse cried out: Justly I am judged by God and I am damned. Whereupon everyone was terrified that a man of such accomplishments could be lost. A certain [man] among them, Bruno, addressed his students.

Only the last words of the text refer to Bruno's address to his students. Standing at the city gate, he points the way. The illuminator, probably Jean de Limbourg, has not scrupled to give Bruno darker gray hair and quite different features from those in Paul's preceding or subsequent miniatures. The Carthusian life is a combination of Western monasticism with the eremitical tradition of Egyptian solitaries and here the magic power of Bruno's words has conjured up for his students a distant view of clear symbols of the future. Hermits in their caves and a lonely tomb foretell the life of solitude, and the road leads up to a large portal that foreshadows the institution of a religious order.

The color is less balanced and less subtle than in the preceding miniature by Paul. The figures, though statuesque and probably designed by Paul, are more simply articulated and, as usual in Jean's paintings, the landscape completes their rhythmical pattern.

Fol. 96   The Vision of Bishop Hugh.

What hope is there for us, miserable as we are? Let us flee and live in a solitary place. On reaching Burgundy, they went to a certain bishop of saintly life who, in a dream, had seen them coming in the form of seven stars falling before him.

The Bishop of Grenoble, wearing his miter in bed, lies dreaming. The seven stars that foretell the arrival of Bruno and his six followers are clustered against the curtain suspended from golden rings on the far side of the bed. Nearer us the corresponding curtain is bound into a roll, so that the room is visible through the open double arch. The painter has provided a bedside chair and a strange little hexagonal object at whose use we can only guess. Outside the chamber, which is seen from the right, there is a section of a chapel, and, at the left, a wall which extends forward to give an unconvincing sense of depth. The statue on the capital, wearing a miter, identifies the building as episcopal.

The color is exceptional and bold. The painter has juxtaposed two large areas of quite similar red and scarlet, separating them only by the white sheet and the very beautiful slate-blue curtain. These zones of strong color are then embedded in a large area of limpid light green.

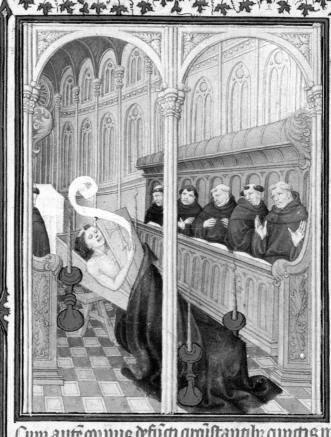

Cum aute corpus defuncti arrcustantibz cunctis m
sepulcro poni debet clamauit dicens. Justo dii iudicio
arrusatus sum. quo audito unuusi q assabant
stupesti corp ad ecclam portat scrasturu refuuantes.

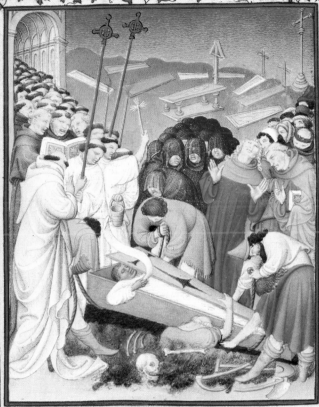

Sequenti die exequijs celebratis mortuus uer
clamat. Justo dñ iudicio iudicatus sum tñc mag̃
admirati quia iudicañ sonare potest i bonñ ul'
malu deliberanest expectare i crastinu uim reseruãtes

Mane facto congatis omnib; ad sepliedum
mortuū iteru clamat. Justo dni iudicio 2 dempnat
sum. vnde pteriti sunt omis ꝙ uir tantc sāc
pdit eēt et ex quib; bruno scolares suos alloquit.

Quid nos miseri sp̄ire debemus ecce fugiam? et
h̄itemus ĩ solitudine et puemetes ad burgũdi
am acceleunt qũedã epm sc̄e uite qui uenie
tes ĩ sōpnio uidat ut by. stellas ãi se cadente?

Et pea p diuersos montes ascendentes usq; lo2
quedam hozridu et ab hominibz remotu ubi se
arestaurint qui intellecta causa qua ibidem
ueniat dixit eis sao nob locu a deo paratum.

Fol. 96v   Bishop Hugh receiving Bruno and his Companions.

And after having crossed various mountains until [they reached] a certain [place], wild and distant from mankind, where they stopped; there [the bishop] understanding why they came to that very spot said: I know the place prepared for you by God.

On reaching Burgundy Bruno and his six companions visited the Bishop of Grenoble to seek his counsel on a suitable site for their settlement. They kneel before Bishop Hugh who, dressed in full pontificals, raises a gloved hand to bless an old friend. He recognizes that the seven stars of his dream were prophetic, and he says that God has revealed to him the chosen place.

The building resembles the one in the *Dream,* although here it is seen from the left. Behind the bishop, furthermore, a barrel-vaulted chapel ending in a glazed window opens out of the chamber.

The color is as beautiful as in the preceding miniature, but quieter. Within a large area of pale green the painter has subtly blended violet, brown, pink, white, and one of the exquisite blues of which the Limbourgs were masters. The rose on the miter and crosier are no less delightful.

And, not without great effort, he led them to the place where the seven stars he had seen in a dream rested, and he said: This will be your place. Accordingly there, during the lifetime of the saintly bishop, they began to construct the first house of the Carthusian Order.

Through the very portal evoked by Bruno's address to his students on leaving Paris (95v) the companions enter the monastic church they have built. Most of the Carthusians now wear the characteristic wide scapular all of a piece with the cowl and held at the sides by a broad band. One monk clothed in the habit is already in the church. Bruno follows, bending forward and clasping his hands to express both eagerness and reverence. Behind him a companion slips on his tunic. Paul de Limbourg—for it was surely he who designed and painted this magnificent miniature—has contrived to combine exceptionally large, heavy, monumental figures with a superb rhythmical movement into the building. To accomplish this he was willing to sacrifice a little more of the structure and plastic independence of his figures than would have seemed desirable to major Italian masters, for they insisted on an individual axis in each of them. Paul's models in this instance were the statues of Claus Sluter, particularly those in the portal at Champmol.

No painter of the period could have equaled the splendor of Paul's modulation of white, although it is true that such delicate luminosity would have been largely lost over the centuries in panel and mural paintings, which are exposed to surface abrasion and to light. Paul's decision to represent one man just pulling on his white tunic and behind him a companion still without it tells us much about his logical way of composing a scene. This companion, already tonsured, is evidently one of the two laymen who set out with Bruno and who has not yet completed his novitiate. Paul has given him a color probably not worn by Carthusian novices at that time but which repeats the beautiful blue of the script.

Et eos non sine grandi labore ad locum ubi. vij.
stelle q̃s uidat in sopnio steterat dixit et ait. hic
eut locus uester: ibi igitur ipo epo uiuo sc̃o uiuã
te edificare cepit pm̃a domũ ordis cartusiensiũ.

Que domus cartulia uero nomine nuncupa
tur itia artos montes burgundie secundum illud uero
opidum in caurer est solitudo paradisus. Pax
est in cella fons instant iurgia bella.

Fol. 97v   The Grande Chartreuse.

This house, called in truth the Charterhouse, is situated among the serried mountains of Burgundy; according to Jerome: the city is a prison, the desert paradise. In the cell is peace; strife and war threaten without.

The last miniature in the cycle shows the monastery that Bruno and his companions founded. The site of the Grande Chartreuse, which is not very far from Grenoble, is not very far either from Vienne, where the most important relics of St. Anthony, one of Bruno's models, were held. A disastrous fire of 1371 swept away the buildings, and the king as well as princes of the blood and the 550 Carthusian houses contributed to the reconstruction of the mother house of the Order. Though the mountainous terrain in the miniature suggests Grenoble, and the chapel on the hill probably represents the one built above the monastery by Bruno, the main buildings may not depict the Grande Chartreuse but a characteristic charterhouse with a separate habitation for each monk opening on to a cloister. The Duke of Berry was, in fact, a patron of the Chartreuse de Vauvert in Paris. He built a chapel there for a reliquary to contain the head of his name saint, John the Baptist.[3]

The disproportionately large church and the uncoordinated perspective disturb the unity of the miniature. Brown eagles high on the peaks reinforce the wildness and solitude of the place; the Grande Chartreuse is still known as "le desert." A large white bird resembling the Duke's swan rests on the steeple.

The only visible men, lay brothers or *Donates,* are on or near the glistening water. Three of them fish. This is not an idle occupation, because total abstinence from meat is a distinctive mark of the Order; but the Rule permits fish on occasion, even to the degree that it may be bought, if necessary, for a monk who is ill.

The Office of the Dead was often said in choir over a dead body. For a century that text had been illustrated in French Books of Hours by a service around a bier. The first miniature to depart from that long established tradition was this startling and dramatic scene. It is reminiscent, to a degree, of the *Burial of Diocrès* (95). In a cemetery filled with crosses and tombstones two hermits quietly read or pray from large tomes. Between them a strange bust, probably of a prophet, appears behind a white tablet fixed to a pink column below a crucifix of the same color. Looking at one of the hermits the prophet points at the blank tablet and possibly also at the grave below. In this grave lie two wasted corpses, perhaps identifiable as male and female. There are small piles of earth around the edges of the excavation. On the grass between it and the frame lie the tools of grave-diggers as well as a skull and some bones that have recently been dug up.

Has the grave been freshly dug, and will the corpses, newly laid in it, soon be buried? If so, why are the bodies so wasted and the heads nothing but grinning skeletons? Could the corpses have been exhumed? Were they, for special sins, removed to a grave outside the cemetery? Why is the surface of the tablet blank? In a copy of this miniature by the Rohan workshop the crucifix has been moved down to fill the empty tablet.

Many details in this novel composition cannot now be confidently interpreted. Lombard illustrations of this Office, which Paul surely knew, commonly showed a skeleton or the Three Living and the Dead. The famous expanded version of this theme in the Camposanto in Pisa included, above the decayed bodies and the frightened noblemen, hermits quietly reading in the landscape, entirely devoted to contemplation of divine truth. The central figure in Paul's miniature might be, therefore, Macarius, who points the moral in this scene. Perhaps, however, he is Job, who is prominent in the text of the Office of the Dead, or Judas Maccabeus, whose thoughts about the value of intercession to free the dead from sin (2 Maccabees 12: 43–46) influenced Christian doctrine and are, in fact, quoted in the Epistle for the Mass of All Souls in the *Belles Heures.*

Apart from the warm, "hopeful" reds on the crucifix and the books the colors are quite dun, but they are enlivened by countless tiny spots of pink, orange, and blue.

nant Placebo. psalmus   noem oracionis mee.

...len quoni   Qua mclinauit

...am exaudi   aurem suam michi:

...et dominus   et in diebus meis in

This miniature begins the cycle of the Hours of the Passion. After the Last Supper Christ went forth to the garden of Gethsemane. Within the garden, bounded by a wattle fence, he kneels in prayer. His impending death is symbolized by the gold chalice, the Communion wafer, and the small cross that floats between him and God the Father.

Having ended his prayer, Christ returned to the apostles, crossing the plank that bridges the brook of Cedron. According to the contemporary pilgrim Ogier d'Anglure this was the little bridge that had once been composed of the wood of the Cross, and indeed Paul had marked the plank with a cross in his miniature of the Agony of Gethsemane in the *Bible moralisée.*[4]

Christ comes to rouse the slumbering apostles and to warn them of the impending betrayal. A serpent creeping out of a crevice perhaps foretells the arrival of Judas with the soldiers, who will soon approach down the road from Jerusalem. Deeply sorrowful, Christ bends and lays his hand gently on James. Peter, wrapped in his blue cloak, is propped on one arm, his hand near the pommel of a sword he has brought to defend his master. John, a mere youth, has fallen into a deep sleep and leans heavily on the older disciple.

The beauty of the intertwined volumes of these figures implies a design by Paul. They are united, too, with Christ by the conical hill behind. Its rippling surface as well as the curling folds in the violet mantles and the repeated curvatures in the composition as a whole suggest the taste of Jean. The brook of Cedron winds around the hill, its waves represented by strokes of yellow and transparent green over gold. The entire scene glows with yellow and gold. It is the most sophisticated and most perfect miniature by Jean in the manuscript.

Fol. 123v   The Betrayal. *Matins.*

"Judas then, having received a band of men and officers from the chief priests and Pharisees, cometh thither with lanterns and torches and weapons" (John 18: 3). Judas, usually shown in profile, approaches Christ from behind to give the kiss, which was a prearranged signal. Peter, who has cut off the ear of Malchus, obeys the command of Christ to return his sword to its scabbard. Christ reaches out to touch and heal the wounded ear. The dour faces, disjointed figures, and flat design without clear spatial intervals disclose the authorship of Herman. Paul, however, may have provided a model for Peter and Malchus.

Fol. 124   Christ before the High Priest. *Matins.*   HERMAN

"And they that laid hold on Jesus led him away to Caiaphas the high priest . . . and all the council sought false witness against Jesus to put him to death" (Matthew 26: 57,59). Caiaphas, wearing a miter and holding a sword of justice, listens to the false evidence that Christ has claimed that he could destroy the temple and build it up again within three days. The illuminator has not well unified the two groups, leaving an awkward space between them. Herman's conception of Christ is not memorable, and he has covered the throne of the priest, with its characteristic Limbourg motifs of disks and acanthus, with a very strange canopy of pointed stakes.

Fol. 131v   Christ mocked. *Lauds.*   HERMAN

"Then did they spit in his face, and buffeted him; and others smote him with the palms of their hands . . ." (Matthew 26: 67). Caiaphas, again wearing a miter and now holding a crozier, sternly surveys the scene. The green arcade echoes the lively actions of the soldiers. The color is interesting and distinctive: orange-red, pink, plum, golden brown, and a blue of different quality than we have seen, all favored by Herman. The faces show his typical pug noses, flat features, and scowling mouths.

Fol. 132   The Flagellation. *Lauds.*   HERMAN

A short officer, strutting like a cock, and two underlings wield scourges while a youth
raises a birch high above his head. A kneeling assistant pulls on the rope that holds
Christ to the column. The painter's oddly proportioned figure of Christ is more
pathetic than noble. Perhaps the man at the right wearing a tiara and looking at the
scene with conspicuous determination is Pilate. Herman, who could never resist
strange headgear, has provided the high priest's companion with a fantastic red Mon-
golian hat. The painter matched this miniature with the facing *Mockery* by introducing arches above, upraised arms, an overseer at the right, a tiled floor, and related colors.

Fol. 135v   Christ before Pilate. *Prime.*   HERMAN

A kneeling soldier eagerly repeats the accusations to the Roman governor, who sits on
a throne like that of Caiaphas on folio 124. Its size and height relate it to the building
on the facing page. Pilate raises an admonitory finger before Christ, who is held in the
grasp of mailed fists. The emotion of the moment is conveyed by a banner that flutters
over his head. The burning taper reminds us of the early morning hour. A small area of
Herman's favorite deep blue-green landscape is visible behind Pilate's hand.

Fol. 136   Pilate offers to release Christ. *Prime.*   HERMAN

Pilate, in one of Herman's curving hats, addresses the Jews, offering in accordance with
custom to release one prisoner at Passover. They ask not for Christ but Barabbas. One
dramatic Hebrew at the center, arm flung up in excitement, is entirely averted. Since
the Jews could not enter Pilate's judgment hall before the Passover for fear of ritual
defilement the governor speaks from a high exterior pulpit. To accommodate it part
of the ivy border has been erased. At the barred prison window appear the two crimi-
nals who shared crucifixion with Christ.

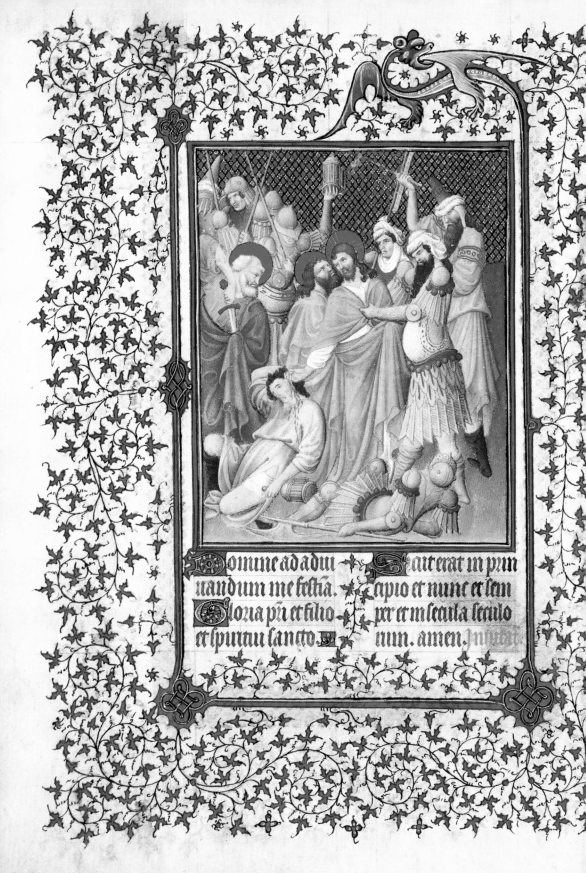

omine ad adiu
uandium me festla.
Gloria pri et filio
et spiritui sancto.

ait erat in prin
cipio et nunc et sem
per et in secula seculo
rum. amen. Insipit.

Regem xpm adua
ſinum dominū
nenite adoremus.
Pſalmus

Venite exultem
domino iubi
lemus deo ſalutari n
ro preocupemus fa

Deus in
adiuto
rium me
um intende

Domine ad adiuua
dum me festina
Gloria pri et filio et
spiritu sancto.

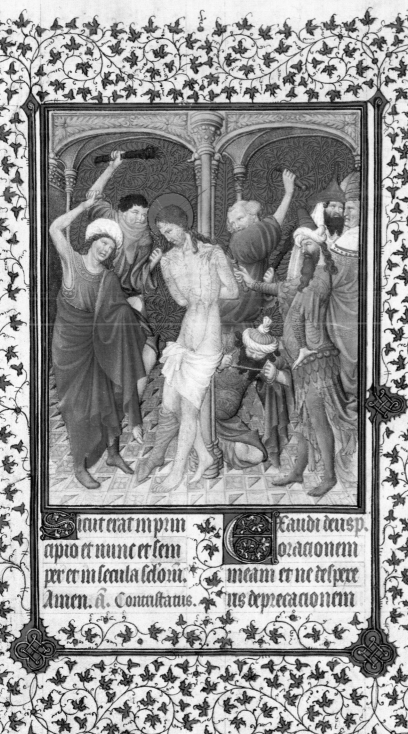

Sicut erat in prin
cipio et nunc et sem
per et in secula sclorum.
Amen. A. Contristatus.

Exaudi deus p.
orationem
meam et ne despere
us deprecationem

eus in ad-
iutorium
meum in-
tende

Domine ad adiu-
uandum me festia
Gloria pri et filio
et spiritui sancto

Siat erat in prin
aipio et nunc et semp
et in seaila seaulorum.
amen. Hympnus.

nqui uelatu
facie finctisol
iustiae fleris illusus
gentibus cesus quoqz

"When he [Pilate] was set down on the judgment seat, his wife sent unto him, saying, Have thou nothing to do with that just man: for I have suffered many things this day in a dream because of him ... When Pilate saw that he could prevail nothing ... he took water, and washed his hands before the multitude, saying, I am innocent of the blood of this just person" (Matthew 27: 19, 24).

Surrounded by soldiers Christ awaits Pilate's decision. His wrists are bound and the long sleeves of his blue robe cover his hands, so that he appears entirely helpless. Pilate holds his hands over a golden basin as a servant pours water over them from a ewer—a public disclaimer of responsibility. His wife, who has failed to persuade him to dismiss the prisoner, leans out from behind the throne. Medieval authors, following Hrabanus Maurus, envisaged her as a tool of the devil, who sent her a dream in a last effort to prevent Christ's death on the cross and thus to thwart the plan of salvation.

Herman has again given Pilate a hat that looks like an exotic bloom. Indeed the entire composition seems flowery, with its array of bright red, pink, pale green, and warm brown lighted in golden yellow. To achieve recession the painter as usual set a large form at an angle, but he has not clearly envisaged spatial intervals between the figures. Herman's flat-faced men have their habitual grim look. In their company the malevolent old man in a rose and white mantle intently watching the scene is exceptionally expressive.

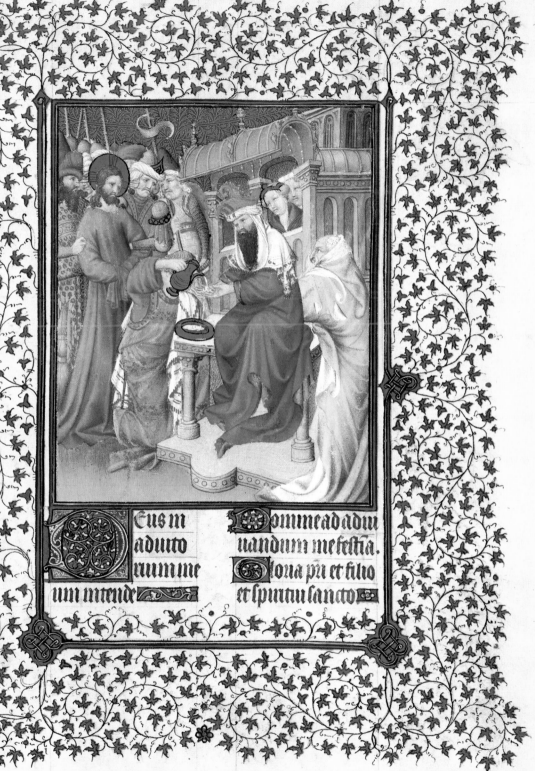

Eus in adiutorium meum intende

Domine ad adiuuandum me festina. Gloria pu et filio et spiritui sancto

Sicut erat in pn̄ / cipio et nunc et sem / per et in secula seculo / rum. Amen. Ymnus̄

Hora qui ductu / Dentria fuisti ad / supplicia x̄ƥe ferendo / humeris cuutem pro

Fol. 138v   Way to Calvary. *Terce.*   HERMAN

The Virgin attempts to lighten Christ's burden by supporting the cross. He turns a sorrowful face toward her, but a soldier intervenes. The other brightly colored soldiers
sounding a horn or raising a banner transform this sad journey into a pageant. Herman,
to be sure, does not synchronize well at this time the movement of the several parts of
a figure. Christ, like the soldiers, has the loose, limp character of a puppet. The dis-
emboweled body of Judas dangles from a tree before a deep blue background of the
kind that Herman greatly favored.[5]

Fol. 141v   Christ nailed to the Cross. *Sext.*   HERMAN

In an apparently unique passage in the French version of Jean de Berry's *Meditations*
God the Father warned Christ that he would need to redeem Adam's action of reaching
for the apple and stepping toward the tree by being stretched upon the cross and
attached with three nails, "rough, badly forged, and blunt at the end."[6] Such a nail lies
here. Christ looks up steadfastly at the devil, hovering with outstretched claws in
expectation that redemption may yet fail. The drawing of an unpainted crown of
thorns is visible on the ground.[7]

Fol. 142   Christ offered the Sop. *Sext.*   HERMAN, WITH PAUL

"And one ran and filled a sponge full of vinegar, and put it on a reed, and gave him to
drink" (Mark 15: 36). The centurion points at the dying Christ. The seated Virgin and
the unusual, averted St. John stand out as fully realized volumes before the rather flat
figures behind. The model or drawing for them, and perhaps even part of the execution,
must be ascribed to Paul. The Limbourgs introduced shields in the form of grotesque
masks into the earlier *Bible moralisée*, but none as expressive as this wailing face.

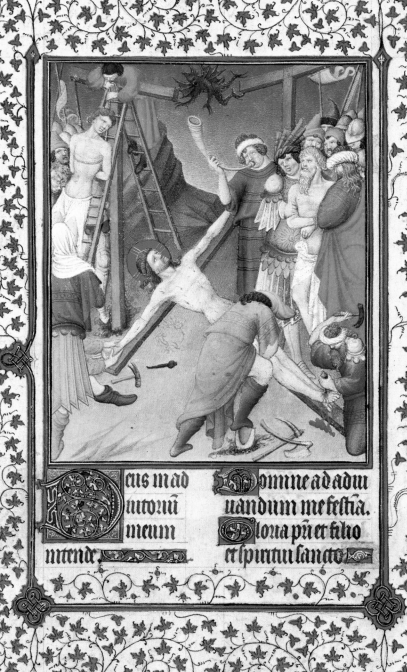

eus ma ad   omine ad adiu
iutoriu   uandum me festia.
meum   loria pri et filio
intende   et spiritui sancto

Sicut erat in prin
cipio et nunc et sem
per et in secula sdok
Amen. Ympnus.

rucem pro
nobis subijt
et stans in illa sint
ibus saaatis mam

"But when they came to Jesus and saw that he was dead already, they brake not his legs: But one of the soldiers with a spear pierced his side, and forthwith came there out blood and water" (John 19: 33, 34).

The soldiers did break, however, the limbs of the two thieves. Herman incorporated into the miniature an incident from the *Golden Legend,* not commonly represented. Longinus, the centurion who pierced Christ, suffered from a disease of the eyes. Here he raises his spear with lowered lids, and the hands of two comrades help to direct the thrust. His disease was cured by the blood that flowed from the wound.

One of the soldiers again holds a shield in the form of a grotesque mask. At the foot of the cross a guard leaning on his spear has turned away from the sight of the mutilated dead. We are told that soldiers cast lots for Christ's seamless garment, and here a group of three, oblivious of the scene behind them, could well be occupied with dice. One of them turns his back to the beholder.

Herman again has employed his favored reds, pinks, blues, and yellow-browns. The blue tunic of one soldier bears small, sparkling golden motifs of the sort Herman usually included in his background; they give the figure a disproportionate prominence.

Deus mad
iutonum
meum in
tende.

Domine ad adiu
uandum me festia.
Gloria pri et filio
et spiritui sancto

Sicut erat in prin
cipio et nunc et sem
per et in secula secu
lorum. Amen. vii.

eata xpisti
passio sit nostra
liberacio et per hanc
nobis gaudia para

"Now from the sixth hour there was darkness over all the land unto the ninth hour. And about the ninth hour Jesus . . . when he had cried again with a loud voice, yielded up the ghost . . . and the earth did quake, and the rocks rent; and the graves were opened and many bodies of the saints which slept arose . . . Now when the centurion, and they that were with him, watching Jesus, saw the earthquake, and those things that were done, they feared greatly saying, Truly this was the Son of God" (Matthew 27: 45–54).

This awesome event, described only by Matthew, is Herman's second subject for None. According to St. Luke (23:45) the sun was darkened, and the scene is bathed in an unearthly blue-gray light, such as falls on the earth during an eclipse (a nearly total one was visible in northern France in 1406). Into the gloom strikes a shaft of supernatural light. Rocks have been split and three of the dead emerge through cracks in the earth, raising their hands in supplication. An armed guard at the foot of the cross, still grasping his spear, falls back against his terrified comrades. The kneeling centurion and a group of spectators look up in amazement toward the source of the yellow and red light that passes behind the repentent thief and comes near the side of the crucified Savior.

No earlier painting had offered so impressive a depiction of darkness at noon. Herman created his nocturne by developing the common mode of grisaille. He laid his blue-gray strokes over a somewhat lighter ground, producing a kind of shimmer. This ground is warmer and lighter in the flesh areas, and brick-red in the falling guard. The same red lies in the shadows of the mantle of the kneeling centurion. Herman here proves to be a subtle and resourceful painter.

Fol. 149 The Deposition. *Vespers.* JEAN

"And now when the even was come . . . Joseph of Arimathaea, an honourable counsellor, which also waiteth for the kingdom of God, came, and went in boldly unto Pilate and craved the body of Jesus . . . And he bought fine linen and took him down" (Mark 15: 42–46).

As usual in representations of the Deposition the feet of Christ are still fastened to the cross while the body is lowered. Joseph, on the lower rungs of his ladder, supports the corpse from below and Nicodemus, higher up, holds fast to the transverse beam while steadying the corpse with his left arm. The mantle that covered the Virgin's head in earlier scenes has fallen back, and the very youthful mother looks up tenderly and reaches out to receive her son, whose right arm has fallen limply upon her shoulder. On the opposite side Mary Cleophas, wearing a white wimple and a striking scarlet and gold mantle, holds the Crown of Thorns in her reverently covered hand. She is accompanied by the Magdalen in green shaded in blue and a young man who brandishes the two nails.

The figures compose a beautiful arabesque, strengthened by the ladders, the cross, and the twin peaks in the distance. Jean's design is here at once bolder and simpler than those of Herman. He modulates surfaces more subtly, giving them the kind of polish we observed in the *Agony*. A greater sensitiveness is apparent also in the figures, especially the Virgin Mary.

eus in ad
iutorium
meum in
tende.

Domine ad adiu
uandum me festina
Gloria pri et filio et
spiritui sco.

Sicut erat in principio et nunc et semper et in secula seculorum Amen. ā. Miserere p.

Miserere mei domine miserere mei quin in te confidit anima mea.

The subject of the Lamentation acquired a new prominence in the art of the late Middle Ages. The vision of the naked, wounded corpse of Christ stretched on the ground below the cross realized more vividly than any other representation the new sense of the tragedy of death in the world, even that of the Son of God as part of the plan of redemption. The scene also provided an unequaled opportunity to depict the impact of Christ's death upon his mother, his close relatives, and his friends. The Lamentation had thus been added earlier to cycles of the Passion in Italy. This miniature is apparently the first example by a French painter, but a few years earlier the scene was introduced by an Italian illuminator into the *Brussels Hours* of the Duke of Berry, a manuscript that the Limbourgs knew well.

Although Paul did not adopt the composition of that miniature his imposing figures and geometric design disclose again the depth of his understanding of Italian painting. He no doubt found the mourner who bends forward and tears her hair in Simone Martini's panel of the Entombment, now in Berlin but then probably at Dijon, the Burgundian capital which he certainly had visited. Paul was impressed also by the movement of Simone's St. John, who covers his grief-stricken face with his mantle. Paul's St. John maintains the idea of concealment by laying a hand on his face—an equally unusual and expressive gesture. It may once again have been the *Brussels Hours* that suggested to Paul the dramatic foreshortened figure of the Magdalen, which Jacquemart there introduced into the *Entombment*. The more dramatic Magdalen in the *Belles Heures* kisses the feet, not a hand, of Christ. The foreshortening, too, is more drastic. We have seen similarly foreshortened figures in other miniatures by Paul (19, 73v, 74).

Paul's knowledge of Trecento painting was so profound that he could improvise *all'italiana*. If he was inspired by a specific prototype for the woman who lays a comforting hand on the Virgin's head we have so far been unable to find it. The significance of her solicitude is increased by her size and her bearing—a remarkably majestic figure. The Virgin alongside seems small. Eyes closed, she slumps, without hope, letting the arm of Christ lie limply in her left hand, while with her right she has raised her mantle as if to wipe the tears. Entirely drained of vitality, she yet remains the central figure. Hers is the strongest color, and the movements turn about her like the spokes of a wheel. It is to her that the companions (except the Magdalen) are related. The body of Christ, partially rolled away, is left largely alone.

Christ is lowered slowly into the tomb. Joseph of Arimathaea supports the torso, an assistant in a rose mantle bends down to take the weight of the legs, and a man in a turban kneels at the feet and pulls on the winding sheet. The mourner in a drab green mantle holds the necessary spices in a golden box. At the head of the tomb one of the holy women holds the Crown of Thorns, which later became the most precious relic of the Sainte-Chapelle in Paris. The Virgin kneels, supporting her son's arm. She is as pale as the lifeless hand she presses against her cheek, reluctant to let it go. The intense blue of her mantle and that of Joseph frame the corpse. The wild despair of the Magdalen contrasts with the quiet sorrow of the Virgin below her. She throws back her head and, like a mourner in the *Lamentation,* tears at the long golden hair which she had once used to wipe the Savior's feet. The jagged peak behind echoes her agitation.

The violet of the Magdalen's mantle repeats, at a deeper level, the color of the tomb, and leads the eye back through a gap between the figures into the landscape beyond. Almost all of these powerful figures seem to have been designed and painted by Paul. The men in red, however, near Christ's feet are singularly weak, probably because of a rather surprising allocation to Herman.

Fol. 152v   Sleeping Soldiers beside the Tomb. *Compline.*   HERMAN

"Now the next day . . . the chief priests and Pharisees came together unto Pilate, saying, Sir, we remember that that deceiver said, while he was yet alive, After three days I will rise again. Command therefore that the sepulchre be made sure until the third day . . . Pilate said unto them, Ye have a watch: go your way, make it as sure as you can" (Matthew 27: 62–65).

The three soldiers have fallen asleep around Christ's solitary tomb, but to a degree they still guard it. The averted soldier is half upright, his hand resting on the pommel of his sword. The head of a comrade has fallen forward on his knee, but he still has hold of his grotesque shield in a form of a mask with wide-open mouth (like the famous *Bocca della Verità* in Rome). The guard with a battle-axe sleeps with his hand on the lid.

Herman, no doubt following Paul, has painted a deep landscape. Trees rise from the hills beyond the barren foreground. The city of Jerusalem dominates the heights to the right, and against the horizon the thieves still hang on their crosses on the more distant, and therefore also lighter, Mount Calvary. This is one of the earliest examples of a sky streaked with clouds.

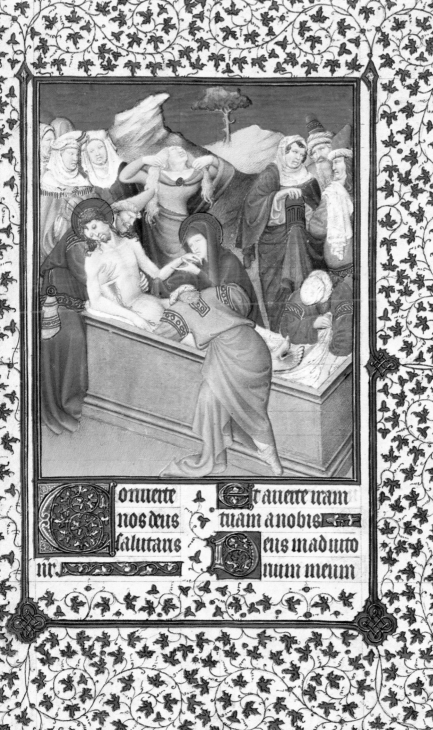

onuerte
nos deus
salutaris
nr.

Et auette iram
tuam a nobis.

Deus mad intto
num meum

intende · · · ſpūtui ſancto.

Omine ad adiu / iaut erat in prin

uandium me festina / apio et nunc et ſeper

Gloria pri et filio et / et in ſecla ſeculorum.

Oremus. Oracio.

Deus qui corda
fidelium sa
spiritus illustracione
docuisti: da nobis in
eodem spiritu recta
sapere et de eius sem
per sancta consola
cione gaudere. per.

De sancto spiritu. ant.

Ueni sancte spus
reple tuorum
corda fidelium et tui amo
ris in eis ignem accendes
Emitte spiritum tuum
et creabuntur. Rm.
Et renouabis facie
terre. Domine exaudi
oracione meam. Et cla
mor meus ad te ueniat.

Beata dei genitrix
et benedicta tuum

Fol. 155   Pentecost and Trinity.

The suffrages begin with prayers calling for the intercession of the Holy Spirit and the Trinity. The descent of the Holy Spirit had already been illustrated in Paul's miniature for the Hours of the Holy Spirit on 84, but the text here, *Veni sancte spiritus*, is the versicle for Pentecost Sunday and no other subject would have been appropriate.

It may at first seem strange that the painter should have further restricted his limited space by setting his interior back from the picture plane and framing it within a wide, luminous pink arch, but the resulting perspective creates the illusion of a wider space. By an unusual design, moreover, he has used the foreground to increase the illusion of depth. The Virgin and disciples are seated within an enclosure that extends forward at an angle to touch the lower edge of the frame. The dove and golden rays descend through an opening at the center of the vault—a device the Limbourgs had already introduced in their Bible to admit supernatural forms to an earthly interior.

In the Trinity God the Father holds within his embrace the Son of Man and—last in time to be revealed—the Holy Spirit, who is represented as a youth. The face of Christ, a bearded man, bears signs of suffering. All three are dressed alike and the Father's encircling cloak binds them together and cradles the open book, which, with his drapery, serves as a kind of ship floating upon the clouds. As so often in the miniatures of the Limbourgs the rose of the book and the blue of the sky are combined in the violet of God's mantle to create a beautiful harmony of color. Possibly they hold the Book of Life containing the names of the blessed (Revelation 20: 12–15) though it could equally well represent the scriptures with the progressive revelation of the Trinity. There are two other miniatures of the Trinity in the *Belles Heures* (91v, 204) but this image, in the form as it were of the three ages of man—youth, maturity, and old age—is certainly the most original.

Fol. 156   Heraclius returning with the Cross.   JEAN AND HERMAN (?)

In about A.D. 600 Chosroes, King of the Persians, set fire to the holy places and carried off the wood of the Holy Cross into Persia. The Emperor Heraclius proceeded against him and, having defeated Chosroes, led the Christians with the Holy Cross back to Jerusalem.

The miniature represents the event described by the text beneath the next miniature. The Emperor, "arrayed in regal attire," could not enter the gate of the city because it swung closed before him. The horses are brought up short and the groom turns for help to the Emperor, who rides in the covered wagon. In all these respects the miniature resembles closely the representation on a medal bought by the Duke in 1402 and probably made by a Parisian goldsmith—perhaps the very one to whom Jean and Herman were apprenticed in 1400. During the period 1400–1402, furthermore, the Byzantine Emperor Manuel II, visiting Paris, became a friend of Jean de Berry. Except for the medal and this miniature all other early representations follow the *Golden Legend* and show the Emperor on a charger. Early Italian paintings include an angel above the closed gate who, according to the same source, reminded Heraclius that Christ had entered riding a lowly ass. His upward glance in the miniature implies that the Limbourgs either knew such paintings or were familiar with the *Legend*.

Fol. 156v   Heraclius enters Jerusalem.   HERMAN WITH PAUL

When, arrayed in regal attire, he wanted to enter the city-gate through which Christ went out bearing his Cross the gate mysteriously closed; on the other hand it opened to him when he humbled himself. Hence the solemnity of the Exaltation of the Cross.

The Emperor has cast off his royal robes and the gates now open to admit him. In volume and articulation he is a far more impressive figure than his followers, who resemble the puppet-like figures of Herman in the Passion cycle. Characteristic of Herman, too, are the bulging blue studs in the background. For Heraclius Herman probably had a design by Paul. Bowed beneath the cross, now greatly enlarged to emphasize the analogy with Christ, the Emperor climbs a cobbled road to return it to Calvary. The place of the Crucifixion lay outside the city until Constantine incorporated it into the Church of the Holy Sepulcher. Were the painters so well informed that they represented Christ outside the gate on his way to Calvary on 138v and Heraclius entering the city to reach the same site?

For his composition Herman utilized a convention of water and a bridge outside a gate that Paul and Jean had taken earlier from Italian painting for miniatures in their Bible.

According to the *Golden Legend* Heraclius returned the relic of the Cross to an altar on Calvary and it ascribes to him the hymn sung at Vespers on the feast of the Exaltation: "O Cross more splendid than the stars of Heaven . . ." To convey the splendor and the universal significance of the cross the designer of the composition, probably Paul, decided he needed more space than would be available within the normal rectangular field and therefore he proceeded, as he had done on other folios, to extend an arch into the upper border, cutting away the original vines and here even the head of a dragon. The enormous gold cross inlaid with jewels has the two-armed form usual for reliquaries designed to hold fragments of the True Cross. Standing on a white altar cloth it is surrounded by twelve hanging lamps, similar to those on the medal of Heraclius.

The Emperor—Heraclius himself we may suspect—kneels in adoration, wearing a hat similar to Nero's on 215 and 215v except for an encircling crown, which he could have laid aside out of humility. Long fringed lappets as from a bishop's miter hang beneath it, symbolizing the priestly character of an emperor. A venerable official attends him, wearing a shaggy fur hat, and at his side hangs the strange circular object that appeared earlier on 15v and 156. To the right of the altar kneel two enigmatic figures, perhaps representing the people of Jerusalem who have gathered to celebrate the return of the cross.

Paul probably designed the miniature but the execution seems to have been Herman's. The range of warm and cool colors speaks for him—the vermillion, rose, deep blue, and indigo. Peculiarly his also is the deep green of the landscape.

Although it is not the first of the suffrages the miniature has been given an elaborate border and the gaps in the golden vines have been filled with delicately executed sprays of small red, blue, and gold flowers.

Circa annos domini. vj. cosdroe rex psaium sca lo
ca incedit er lignu sce cuicis i psidem dicit cotrac
eraclius iperator iuit qui deuicto cosdroa popu
lu ranu cum sca cruce ibierosolimam reduxit.

Hic dum ornatus regio scemate per portam qui christus
auem bauulas eruit uellet intrare porta diuinit?
clauditur ei quod humiliato rursum aperitur. unde
celebritas exaltacionis sancte cruas istituntur.

Adoramus te xpe
et benedicimus
tibi quia per sanctam crucem
tuam redemisti mundum.

Omnis terra adoret
te deus psallat tibi
Et psalmum dicat
nomini tuo

omine exaudi oroneᵐ
meam.

Et clamor meus ad
te ueniat. Oremus. oꝛo

Deus qui unigeniti filij tui
domini nostri ihesu xpisti
precioso sanguine
uiuifice crucis uexil-
lum sanctificari uo-
luisti concede quesumus eos
qui eiusdem sancte
crucis gaudent hono-
re tua quoque protec-
tione gaudere. Qui
uiuit et regnat deus
per omnia secula se-
culorum. Amen.

Memoria de beata uirgi-
ne maria.

Salue regina mise-
ricordia dulcedo et
spes nostra salue ad te clama-
mus exules filij eue ad te
suspiramus gementes et
flentes in hac lacrima-
rum ualle eya ergo aduocata
nostra illos tuos misericor-
des oculos ad nos conuerte
et ihesum benedictum fructum

f. 157 vᵒ

Fol. 157v   Madonna enthroned. *Commemoration of The Virgin.* JEAN

The Madonna is celebrated by two angels, who sing while sounding a psaltery and a lute. In one respect the composition is exceptional. The naked Child, seated sideways within her mantle, turns to suckle, so that his face becomes largely invisible to the beholder. This posture was not only contrary to medieval canons of representation but in religious legends Christ turned his back to signify the unworthiness of the beholder. In the early fifteenth century, an era of more naturalistic imagery, the informal, averted Child was introduced into Paris by an Italian illuminator, the Brussels Initials Master, who worked for the Duke of Berry. The growth of a new tradition of this kind is especially interesting because of the adoption of the posture by Jan van Eyck in his *Madonna of the Fountain.*

Fol. 158v   St. John the Baptist.   JEAN

The painter has given the patron saint of the Duke a background of deep blue studded with gold fleurs-de-lys. He stands before a semicircle of trees bearing bright red fruit. They share in the radiance that descends on him from above and represent those who have heeded his warning: ". . . every tree that bringeth not forth good fruit is hewn down and cast into the fire" (Matthew 3:10). The book lying at his feet, open at its center, may allude to the special position of the Baptist as a link between the Old and New Testaments—the last of the Prophets and the first of the Evangelists.

A robust man of strong features, John has the traditional shoulder-length hair and untrimmed beard of a Nazarene dedicated to God from birth. A soft pink mantle, somewhat inappropriate for an ascetic, is draped over his tunic of camel's hair. Caught beneath his right elbow, it falls to the ground to break into a swirl against the green grass, counterbalancing the ample folds that in the Byzantine tradition cover the raised hand supporting the lamb.

When Christ appeared on the banks of the Jordan the Baptist cried out "Behold the Lamb of God, which taketh away the sin of the world!" (John 1:29). His words are repeated daily in the sacrifice of the Mass and in the miniature the Lamb responds to his pointing hand by turning its head toward the Precursor.

tto: nomini tuo. Vita.

D omine exaudi oronē
meam. Responsorii.

E t clamor meus ad
te veniat. Oremus. ꝗ

D eus qui oro.
D enuto ordine
angelorum ministia
hominumq; dispen
las concede propicius
ut quib; tibi ministra
tibus in celo assistitur
ab hijs in terra uita
nīa muniamur.
per dominium nrm
ihm xpm filium tuū
qui tecum uiuit et
regnat in unitate ei
dem spiritus sancti ds
pro omnia secula sclor.

De sancto iohē bap. a.

I nter natos mulierū
non surrexit maior
iohanne baptista qui uiā
domino preparauit i deserto.

F uit homo missus
a deo uersus.

C ui nomen erat iohes.

D omine exaudi oronē
meam.

E t clamor meus ad te

Fol. 159v   St. Peter and St. Paul. JEAN

St. Peter and St. Paul are represented together, the two apostles who, according to the antiphon written below the miniature, ". . . loved each other in life and in death were not divided." In accordance with established tradition Paul's beard is long and flowing, Peter's short and square; Paul's crown is domed and bald, Peter has a tonsure and a tuft on his forehead. Both apostles are draped in voluminous cloaks. Peter, holding his key, moves diagonally forward, brushing the inner edge of the frame. Paul, partially overlapped by the frame, stands with upraised sword. His draperies fall from his covered hand in a kind of cascade that the Limbourgs first introduced in their miniatures in the *Bible moralisée.* This and other patterns of their drapery were inspired by the sculpture of Claus Sluter, which they saw at Dijon.

Fol. 161   Martyrdom of St. Bartholomew. PAUL AND JEAN

Nothing in the apocryphal life of the apostle impressed the medieval world so strongly as the manner of his death. Guilds of butchers, tanners, and even bookbinders chose as their patron the saint who had been skinned alive. Earlier in the gathering Paul, who designed and perhaps partly executed this miniature, had extended the rectangular frame upward in an arch by cutting into the gold vines (157). Here, however, the frame was prepared to include the extension that houses the Deity.

The subject is gruesome but the horror is mitigated by the trustful expression of the saint, the beauty and balance of the color, and the serene blue sky, which here replaces the diapered background. The king and his attendants fix their eyes upon Bartholomew, and a youth bending over him pauses in his work as he meets the victim's gaze with a look of compassion. He is given special prominence by the deep violet of his tunic, echoed above in the paler cloth-of-honor behind the Lord. At the head of the trestle table a butcher goes at his work with zest, knife in mouth and holding the table firm with his foot. A second assistant saws away at Bartholomew's leg. With their usual attention to instruments the painters have provided not only a spare knife but a hone. The painting has been abraded below, and we may see the drawing for a foot that was not painted.

Domine exaudi oro
nem meam. ♦♦
Et clamor meus
ad te ueniat. Oremus.
Deus oracio
cuius dextera
beatum petrum apo
stolum ambulan
tem in fluctib; nem
geretur erexit et coa
postolum paulum
tercio naufragante
de profundo pelagi
liberauit exaudi nos
propicius et concede
ut amborum meritis
et utatis gliam ? sequi
mur. Per xpm dnm
nostrum. Amen.
De sco andrea. anti
phona.

aplorum. antipho.
Gloriosi prina
pes terre quomo
do in uita sua dilexerunt
se et in morte non sunt
separati. Vsus
Constitues eos prin
apes sup omnem terram
Memores erunt nomis
tui domine.

f. 159 v°

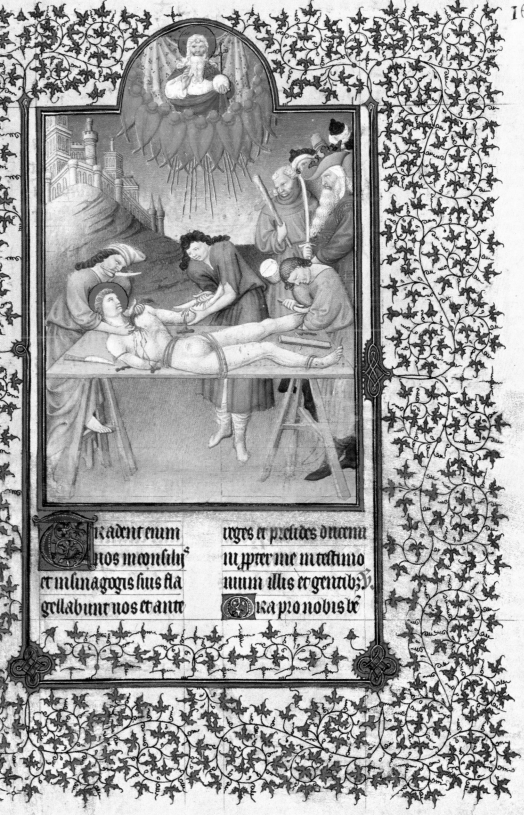

Tradent enim
nos in consilijs
et in sinagogis suis fla
gellabunt nos et ante

reges et presides ducentur
ni ppter me in testimo
nium illis et gentibz.
Ora pro nobis &

Fol. 162 Martyrdom of St. Stephen.

Stephen, a deacon of the Church, was the first to die for the faith. Accused of blasphemy, he was cast out of Jerusalem and stoned to death in the presence of Saul, a fanatical young persecutor known after his conversion as the Apostle Paul. With his legs crossed like Herod ordering the Massacre of the Innocents (59v), Saul sits enthroned holding a curved scimitar.

The design is probably the work of Paul de Limbourg and he himself certainly painted the powerful figures of Saul, the kneeling martyr, and a youth in the foreground, all remarkable for their range of luminous color. Stephen's attackers are less impressive; and the crowded onlookers, with their strange assortment of hats and theatrical expressions, distract from, rather than heighten, the drama. They were probably painted by Herman. God the Father was evidently planned when the border was executed because no other page has an equally wide space between the vines at this place.

Fol. 164v St. Eustace loses his Sons.

Eustace, a commander in Trajan's army, lost his wealth, position, and even his wife after his conversion. Wandering in exile with his young sons he reached a torrent too deep for them to cross. The miniature shows him having brought one across and returning for the other when a lion and wolf carry off both. According to the *Golden Legend* the desperate saint "wept and tore his hair," but Jean, who was certainly the painter, preferred elegance to emotion. Eustace throws up his hands, but not so far as to allow more than the tip of his tunic to fall into the golden waters glazed in green. Mountains frame his head and shoulders and an exceptionally deep landscape stretches away to a distant hill and a light blue sky.

Fol. 165 St. Christopher and the Christ Child.

The painter has resisted the temptation to fill his small space with the many picturesque details of the familiar legend of the patron of travelers. The giant ferryman bends under the weight of the unknown child he expected to carry across so easily. With shoulders hunched and bulging calf-muscles he strains to reach the bank. The text alludes to the divine Child who grasps him firmly as his "crown of precious stones," and the suffrage invokes the saint's protection against maladies of the head.

Cum sanctus martir eustachius
lugeret de filijs in uxore
et filijs suis ab ipso salu

taris rex de celo audit
dicens confide eustachi
eris quippe receptums
morem letus cum filijs

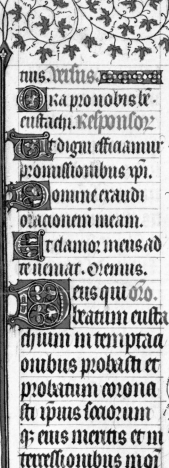

tius. Verlus. Ora pro nobis be
custachi. Responsor
Ut digni efficiamur
promissionibus xpi.
Domine exaudi
oracionem meam.
Et clamor meus ad
te veniat. Oremus.
Deus qui oro.
Beatum eusta
chium in temptaci
onibus probasti et
probatum corona
sti ipsius sociorum
que eius meritis et in
tercessionibus in o
tribulacione tuum
nobis pra auxilii
et sempiterne z sola
cois innunerable gau

dium. Per ipm do
minum nrm. Am.

De sco xpoforo. antha.
Xpofori sci specie
quicunque tue
tur. illo nempe die nul
lo langore tenetur. ð
Posuisti domine sup
caput eius. Responsor.
Coronam de lapide

Fol. 167   St. George killing the Dragon.

The story of a princess offered as willing victim to a monster and saved by a hero is common to both pagan mythology and Christian legend. Differing from Ovid, St. Jerome reported that Perseus had rescued Andromeda not in Abyssinia but at Joppa— the traditional birthplace of St. George, the patron of knighthood. With the struggle to liberate the Holy Places in the Crusades the Christian story assumed a fresh significance. The princess was interpreted as the Church. According to the *Golden Legend* St. George himself appeared when the Crusaders took Jerusalem, his silver armor decorated with the red cross that he bears here on his shield.

Since a helmet was unnecessary against a foe without sword or lance the painter has introduced an angel as a celestial squire to hold it above his head. The dragon, a large realistic crocodile, has been mortally wounded by the shattered lance and the warrior saint turns in the saddle to strike the death blow. His horse seems to aid in the struggle by holding the dragon's tail in his raised foreleg and bringing his rear hoof down on the beast which has passed beneath him. Man, horse, and monster are linked in a circle, bounded by the extremities of the dying dragon below and the curved scimitar above. The princess, watching from the left, kneels in prayer, a white lamb at her side—the only one of her father's flocks not yet sacrificed to the monster.

When this composition, among many others in the *Belles Heures*, was copied in the *Rohan Hours*, the copyist included even such an unusual form as the angel holding the helmet, but he did not accept one iconographic innovation, probably because he did not understand it. He omitted the two small dragons emerging from the cave to hiss in defense of their parent. Perhaps Jean de Limbourg imagined the two offspring as engaging inhabitants of a more natural world, but they might suggest that there is no final victory over evil.

De sancto georgio ã…   cepisset uenerunt ca pa
            um autem beat⁹   docie regionis uiri excel
            georgius in no   lentissimi et sanctum
minine dei martinum re   corpus eius nocturno

Nicholas, Bishop of Myra, was famous even during his lifetime for sudden appearances to those needing help. Here the patron of sailors answers the call of a party of seafarers as their craft, caught in a sudden storm, is about to capsize.

In their sinking ship the desperate travelers look up and raise their hands beseechingly. All efforts to save it have been abandoned. The mast has split, the sail hangs limp, the tiller is unmanned, and the passengers react each in his own way to the apparently hopeless situation. Watched by an old man, a traveler to the left urges a youth over the side into a dinghy. The three could be grandfather, father, and son, who have decided to give the youngest a chance of survival. A white-bearded old man with covered head remains seated and folds his hands resignedly in prayer. A terrified voyager clings to the shattered mast and, behind him, a fellow-traveler, swaying against the list of the ship, throws up his arms in a dramatic gesture. At his side a still, sorrowful face is lifted in supplication. No one seems aware that their prayers have been heard, although Nicholas, on a patch of bright blue sky, is already grasping the lookout. The bishop's draperies stream behind him, adding to the sense of swift movement. The clouds are clearing behind him and a boat on the horizon is already on an even keel.

This vigorous representation of wind and weather is all the more astonishing because clouds and atmospheric phenomena were only just beginning to appear in Northern painting. Perhaps the Limbourgs had seen the fresco in S. Francesco, Siena, in which Ambrogio Lorenzetti, Ghiberti tells us, painted a severe storm.[8]

de sco nicholao. ant.   br le amabilem exibuit.

Anctus dei micho   Ora pro nobis blus
laus pontifica   brate nicholae. R̃m̃.
li decoratus in sua omni   Ut digni efficaamur

Fol. 169   St. Martin with a Beggar.

Martin, the son of a veteran, was conscripted into the Roman army under the Emperor Constantine. The miniature illustrates an event in the life of the young knight that led to his baptism and finally to his entry into the Church. Passing through the gate of Amiens on a winter's day, the *Golden Legend* relates, Martin was importuned by a nude beggar. Unhesitatingly he cut his cloak in two and gave the beggar half.

Paul, who designed the composition, gave it a narrative character that is exceptional at the time. He has hidden the beggar's face behind the horse, so that we must ourselves infer the nature of his response from the visible part of his body—a body naked except for a tattered loincloth and ending in a bandaged stump on a wooden support. Paul has developed the scene further by introducing a second beggar. Despite his appeal for help this man, though old, is strong and vigorous. Dressed in a violet tunic and a wide-brimmed hat he wears a white sling to contain his belongings. A flask lies nearby and he unknowingly discloses his strength by stepping forward briskly, touching his hat and holding out a bowl. The saint has passed him by, however, and the painter seems to suggest that he is something of an imposter.

In a dream Martin saw Christ himself wearing the half cloak he had given to the beggar and he heard him tell the angels that he had received it from Martin the catechumen. Rather oddly the hand holds a cloth that matches not the saint's cloak but his hood. Did the painter make the change for purely pictorial reasons or to suggest a transformation from material to spiritual substance?

The cobbles of the road, pale and indistinct in the foreground, grow smaller and darker as they recede, like similar surfaces in the *Très Riches Heures*. Not everything in the miniature is of equal quality and Paul must have left part of the execution to his brother Jean.

de ſco martino ant. et virginum chorus ga
O quantis luctus pium et gaudete mar
O quanta prea tino et pium eſt fleir
pie lamenta monachoꝛ martinum. ꝟlis.

"When the good friar preached all work was laid aside as if it were a holiday; judges, lawyers and shopkeepers left their occupations to listen. People came running from the fields; the greatest of ladies left their houses and did not hesitate to rise in the night to go on foot by torchlight so as to find a place near the pulpit of the preacher."

Such, according to an early Life, was the eloquence of the saint that he was sent by the founder to extend the Franciscan Order to France.

For his miniature the painter chose a miracle, rarely if ever illustrated before which is said to have taken place in the Duke's own city of Bourges. The crowd was so vast that the preacher decided to speak, as we see here, in the open air. No sooner has he begun than the sky grows dark. Thunderclaps and flashes of lightning announce a storm. Huge hailstones fall from the cloud onto a distant hill. The congregation would have run for shelter but the saint, recognizing the work of Satan, forbids them to move. Anthony raises a hand in blessing and the vanquished devil, clutching a thunderbolt, makes off in a dark cloud. The sky behind him turns to serene blue.

Together with the storm calmed by St. Nicholas (168) this is the most extraordinary meteorological phenomenon described by any contemporary or earlier painter. Although Jean probably had no model for this specific scene he would at least have known representations of the apostles preaching from similar pulpits to congregations seated, as they are here, on the ground. Only the gray-haired man in profile watches the saint as he admonishes the devil, and it is the strong outer line of his rose cloak that holds the troubled group firmly together, near the preacher. His figure interlocks with the young man in pale green and white over lavender who looks up, like the frightened youth behind him, as if at the storm or even the devil. Another member, whose dark curls stand out against his saffron garment, turns his back. Nearest to the pulpit a fat, frightened person sits with covered eyes, preferring not to see. A second friar watches timidly from the shelter of a portal. The brown Franciscan habits are close in color to the furry devil, but he is fluted with red and yellow from the fire and brimstone of his proper abode.

proles hyſpanie   ane fer auctoꝛ gꝛaae
pauoꝛ īfidelıũ   ꝛpi puıuanuım nep
nona lux ytalie nobile   lapſıs neuıe tempꝰ
depoſıtum nobis pꝛdn   breue arditum deſluat

The miniature of the founder of the Franciscan Order has the most elaborate frame of any of the suffrages. It resembles, but is even richer than, the frame for the *Visitation* on 42v, and here, moreover, the spaces between the vines of the border have been filled with stems of small red and blue flowers.

Against a background of gold filigree set with blue faceted studs Christ crucified appears in a deep blue sky streaked with clouds. Blood streams from his wounds and St. Francis has already received the imprint of Christ's sufferings in his hands, feet, and side. The painter, again Jean, has contrasted effectively the attitude of the saint and his companion. Francis sways backward as he looks up, serene and adoring; his gesture is open and relaxed, his palms bearing the stigmata face outward. The disciple seems confused, tense, and frightened. His elbows are held close and he presses his crossed palms against his chest.

Jean chose his deep blue and other colors to match the brown of the Franciscan Order. The heavy stuff of the habit ripples around the kneeling saint as he moves in this intense experience. The folds leave a small gap on the greensward for the tassle of his rope girdle, and they curl away to expose his bleeding feet. His halo has been painted to simulate tooling on gold leaf—a technique that is used in some of the calendar miniatures (2, 4, 12). Small blue flecks in the curve of the green hillside reflect the sky surrounding the cross, and the coral vaults of the building, echoing in color the saint's wounds, draw the eye to the upper left to balance the composition.

The painter has departed from the usual iconography of the Stigmatization in the fourteenth and fifteenth centuries. Wishing to emphasize bodily suffering he has made the blood exceptionally conspicuous, and he has shown only Christ crucified, abandoning entirely the wings of the seraph, normally present to symbolize the divine being.

Stupor et gau   ignea prefentibus trā
dium o uidet   figuratum fratbus
vomo menaum tu nir   in folari fpeae uerrit te
mlie cuuns et auuga   cadriga in te fignis

Louis IX, the saintly ancestor of the Duke, is honored on August 25th, the date of his departure in 1248 from Aigues-Mortes as leader of his first crusade. Among his knights was Jean de Joinville, whose life of the King informs us that both his Queen Marguerite and the papal legate, Eude, a Cistercian, accompanied the expedition. Since the illuminator gave prominence to three figures, the King, a woman, and a monk in white, he clearly intended to represent the first crusade of Louis in 1248. During the second expedition the Queen remained in France.

On his first crusade St. Louis won a great victory, the capture of Damietta, a city near the mouth of the Nile. The illuminator has probably represented the King's fleet as it sailed to the attack. Louis, his crown surmounted, as Joinville described, by a large fleur-de-lys, raises his hands in prayer as the stronghold of the infidel comes into view. Not only the King's ship but the two following vessels fly the royal pennon, perhaps to signify the presence of the King's two brothers. Serried ranks of helmeted soldiers and the masts of other craft create the impression of an imposing force, drawn up in close formation before the attack.

A brisk breeze fills the sails. Although the sky is cloudless the sea is not blue as in other miniatures, perhaps as an indication of the aftermath of a storm that had in fact scattered many of the ships; or could the painter have heard from a traveler about the muddy waters of the Nile delta? Two precipitous rocks towering like an imaginary Scylla and Charybdis mark the entrance to the harbor. Beyond, the sea is darker. Painted in monochrome, the blue towers of Damietta melt into the sky. Nothing about the city seems eastern, unless the tall, staged tower in the foreground is meant to resemble a minaret.

Rex egregie condam rex francie
ludouice pie cum rege glo
rie triumphans hodie pro

pace requie regni eterne
ipsm deprecare. Uersus.
Ora pro nobis beate
ludouice. Responsorium.

Fol. 174   St. Charlemagne.

With a leg extended on one side and his mantle on the other the Emperor almost fills his broad Gothic throne. Heavily bearded, he is a powerful figure. His imperial mantle falls in vigorous plaits, covering the knee on which rests an orb surmounted by a cross, the insignia held by God himself in many miniatures. Arrayed in full armor he gazes at the drawn sword, used to establish and maintain his vast empire. The Valois monarchs, like their predecessors, claimed descent from him as King of the Franks, and—with the adage "The king is emperor within his kingdom"—their independence from the Holy Roman Empire. Charles V went so far as to place a figure of Charlemagne on his scepter, and here the Emperor's shield displayed by an angel impales the lilies of France with the imperial eagle.

In 1402 Jean de Montreuil, a member of the Duke's circle, wrote to the city of Aachen complaining of the prominence given the eagle on their reliquary bust of Charlemagne, whereas the fleurs-de-lys were only painted insignificantly on the base. "As if," he writes, "the Kingdom of France were of small or no importance and Charlemagne had annexed it by the might of the Alemanni instead of the contrary."

Fol. 174v   St. Maurus.

Maurus has been given precedence over his master St. Benedict, who chose him to extend the Order to France. The young abbot is a highly individual and arresting figure. His face, the fleshy features delicately modeled in brown, wears a troubled expression as if he were filled with uncertainty as he sets out bearing the emblems of his new office, a red crosier and a beautiful blue book. Benedictines normally wear black or more unusually white, though no particular color is specified in the Rule. The relics of Maurus were in the Abbey of Saint-Maur-les-Fossés, which possessed a twelfth-century life of the saint—now in Troyes—showing St. Benedict clothed in brown, at least in the early scenes.

Fol. 175   St. Benedict.

The painter has emphasized Benedict the ascetic rather than the severe author of a rigorous Rule. In Italian representations after the time of Giotto he is usually a powerful, stern man with white hair and a full beard. Here, following an older tradition, he is beardless, though he has a growth of stubble around the chin. His red and gold crosier forms a bright contrast against the luminous black of his habit, which falls in long regular folds. Pentimenti can be seen in the thumb of the very large right hand he raises in blessing.

Spes afflictis   salutis kawle senior
amor hostibus   pia suscipe vota tuor
hostia iustitis regula vir   Gloria et honore co
tutis iuris via forma   ronasti eum domine.

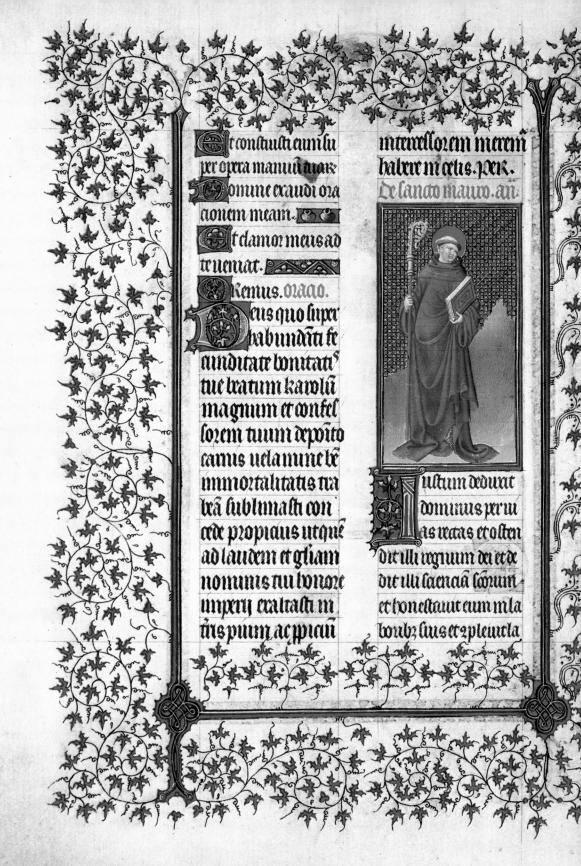

Et construxti eum su
per opera manuû tuaz.

Domine exaudi ora
cionem meam.

Et clamor meus ad
te ueniat.

Oremus. oracio.

Deus quo super
habundâti fe
cunditate bonitatis
tue beatum karolû
magnum et confes
sorem tuum deposito
carnis uelamine ïe
immortalitatis tra
bea sublimasti con
cede propicius utque
ad laudem et gliam
nominis tui honore
imperii exaltasti in
tris puum accipiam

intercessorem merem
habere in celis. per.
De sancto mauro. an.

Iustum deduxit
dominus per ui
as rectas et osten
dit illi regnum dei et de
dit illi scienciam sctorum
et honestauit eum in la
boribz suis et ipleuit la

bones ipius. Verlus
Ra pro nobis beate
maur. Relponlonum.
Ur digni effiaamur
promillionib; xpi.
Omine exaudi ora
nem meam.
Ir damoz meus ad
te ueniat. Oracio
Eus qui eterne
glone partici
pem beatum mauri
abbatem fieri uolui
sti: concede propiciu
ipo intiuenente adi
tum regni celesti cui'
ad beneuiuendum
nos conloztamur
exemplis. Per xpm
dominum nrm. A.
De lancto bndicto an.

ult et oim
turba fidelui
pro glona almi prs
benedicti letentur pre
apue catenie mona
chonum celebzantes ei
festa in terris de quus
societate lancti gaudent
moelis. Plus.
s iulti meditabit

Fol. 177   St. Margaret emerging from the Dragon.

This little miniature with its fine diaper and pale as well as deep, brilliant colors has the richness of an enameled jewel.

Margaret of Antioch was swallowed by the devil in the form of a dragon. When, however, she made the sign of the cross she was saved. No miracle is too unlikely for the author of the *Golden Legend,* but of Margaret's escape from the dragon he says firmly: "This legend is apocryphal and all are agreed that it should be considered a story without foundation."

In the miniature the saint bursts through the monster's back, serene and still praying. She has remained entirely unmarked by the blood that flows to the ground but the danger has not completely passed. The wounded beast lashes with its tail and snaps with its crocodile jaws at her beautiful blue cloak.

At the moment of death Margaret remembered her escape and prayed that if she were invoked infants in difficult births would be brought forth safely. Relics of the saint were popular for this purpose, and written accounts of her life were often placed on women in labor. It is easy to understand Margaret's sympathy with the unborn but mothers may have felt discouraged if they remembered the fate of the dragon!

irgo sancta ka
therina grece
gemma urbe alexandri
na costi regis erat filia. v.
Ora pro nobis beata
katherina. R.
Ut digni efficamur p
millionibus xpi. oro.
Deus qui dedi
sti legem moi
si in summitate mō
tis synai et in eodem
loco per sanctos an
gelos tuos corpus be
ate katherine uirgis
et martiris tue mira
biliter collocasti tribue
nobis quesumus
ut eius meritis et in
cessione ad montem
qui xpus est ualeam

peruenire. per do. no.
De sancta margareta.

kar autem be
ata margari
ta quindecim annorū
ut ab impio olimbrio
tradebatur in carcere. v.
Ora pro nobis bea
ta margareta. Rm.
Ut digni efficamur

Fol. 178v   Martyrdom of the Eleven Thousand Virgins.   HERMAN

Ursula, daughter of the Christian King of Brittany, was betrothed to the pagan heir of the Kingdom of Britain on condition that he accept baptism and send eleven thousand virgins to accompany her to Rome. There the virgins converted and, according to the *Golden Legend*, on the way back they were slaughtered by the Huns at Cologne. That city, represented here on the far side of the Rhine, became the center of their cult and the Duke's inventories include a head sent him by a resident.

Before the *Belles Heures* the martyrdom was commonly represented on land. We know of only three examples of the slaughter in a boat, and Herman, the author of this miniature, probably had not seen them. The little ship is almost identical with that of St. Louis on 173, and it is seen at the same angle. The Rhine looks as vast as the Mediterranean there but, although the spray around the boats is similar, this blue northern river is painted very differently from the muddy waters at the mouth of the Nile. There the waves appear in long vertical ridges perpendicular to the picture plane; here the surface consists of small irregularly placed mounds. Soldiers with expressions typical of Herman press through the gate. The assassins in varied positions strike with their backs turned or look down at their victims. Only one, grasping a virgin as she falls overboard, shows his face. St. Ursula herself, for it is surely she, throws up her hands as she falls back wounded in the breast. A bleeding head lies prominently on the shore, perhaps a tactful reference to the Duke's own relic.

Fol. 179v   St. Lucy beheaded.   JEAN

Jean clearly adopted Paul's composition of St. Catherine beheaded on 19v. Similar are the brilliant blue mantle, the bandaged eyes, and the long blond hair falling heavily as Lucy bows her head for the executioner's stroke. He too has a counterpart, although his upraised arms and the angle of the sword are closer to the headsman in the preceding miniature (19). Even the setting, a green conical hill against a blue and gold diaper, is identical. Yet by changing some elements and simplifying others Jean has transformed the solid and noble Catherine into a more fragile and pathetic martyr.

Et clamor meus ad te
ueniat. Oremus. Oro.
Deus inter cetera potencie tue
miracula ecam in
sexu fragili uictoriã
contulisti : concede
ppicius ut qui beate
agathe natalicia co
limus per eius exem
pla ad te gradiamur.
per xpm dominum
nostrum. Amen
Benedicamus dño
Deo gracias.

De sancta lucia. anт

A tua prouidencia pos
sedisti animam
tuam lucia sponsa
xpi odisti que in mundo
sunt cho uiscas aut ange
lis sanguine ppo imui
cum subisti. Versus.
Ora pro nobis beata
lucia. Rehponsorium.
Vt digni efficiamur p

St. Jerome, neglecting the books of the Prophets to devote himself to [the works] of Plato, was seized by a fever so severe that only in his breast did the warmth of life beat. And [in a dream] avowing himself a Christian before the supreme judgment, the judge [replied]: Thou liest, for [thou art] a Ciceronian.

The longest cycle in the manuscript tells the story of the great scholar and Father of the Church. The first scene, never before represented although it is described in the *Golden Legend,* illustrates how Jerome, sent to study as a young man in Rome and already versed in Greek and Latin literature, grew discontented with the plain un-adorned language of the Scriptures and turned to an intensive study of Cicero by day and Plato by night. The expounder of Plato sits, like Diocrès (94), on his high *cathedra* before a fine lectern. The audience, however, like other audiences in medieval art, is seated on the ground. All but Jerome and his young beardless neighbor are intent on the speaker. The others are mature men, and one—a person of importance in a gold-embroidered pink robe and fur-trimmed hat—raises his hand as if he were about to accompany a comment with a rhetorical gesture. Jerome sits looking down with arms crossed on his breast, already pondering the question that became so trying to the early humanists and which he himself formulated in a letter: "How can Horace go with the Psalter, Virgil with the Gospels and Cicero with the Apostle of the Epistles?"

The painter, influenced by Paul's palette, has used soft, delicate tones. His minia-ture is suffused in a golden light that transforms the more usual rose to peach. When he designed the interior he must have had in mind St. Catherine studying (15). The foreground space is deeper here to accommodate the audience and, since the point of sight has been shifted to the right, only part of the pink-vaulted recess similar to Cath-erine's chapel is visible. Both scholars are seated at lecterns on high thrones placed diagonally before a traceried window. But where Catherine sits back easily, the per-sonification of tranquil study, the professor is perched high in his seat, his soft blue draperies swirling in agitated folds.

Then the Judge ordered a severe beating. Jerome cried out: Lord have mercy on me, if I read these [profane] books again I shall have denied Thee. Then, dismissed, he suddenly regained consciousness in streams of tears and found terrible scars on his shoulders.

The text and the miniature relate the consequences of the dramatic encounter which is described in the preceding title. The Deity, crowned, holding the sword of justice and wearing the priestly pallium, sits enthroned on scarlet cherubim. He points an accusing finger at the untonsured "Ciceronian." Jerome, ready to renounce his beloved authors, now begs for mercy. The flogging is carried out by angels, whose wings repeat the muted green of the tiled floor and of the tawny rush mat below.

Jerome, hand to face in the usual medieval posture of sleep, lies dreaming. Although he is still, his mat is set askew, and he is surrounded by a vast, empty space, the more impressive because the celestial scene occurs nearer the foreground. The depth of the tiled floor, the lack of limits at the sides, and the unimpeded flight of the orthogonals to the horizon evoke a sense of mystery. The Limbourgs used the tiled floor for a lying figure once again—David confronted by an angry Lord (67v, p. 256)— but there it is far less effective.

Jerome made public his resolution taken in a dream, and many years later it was used against him by Rufinus, who ridiculed him for his classical quotations. The saint was not, however, seriously troubled; his attitude to dreams had changed. "Can dreams," he asks, "be used in evidence? . . . How often have I dreamed that I was dead and in the grave . . . How often have I flown over mountains and crossed the seas! Does that mean that I am dead or that wings grow from my sides?"

In a letter to his pupil Eustochium Jerome said that the dream that finally turned him exclusively to the Scriptures took place on his way to Jerusalem, when he was transporting the library of pagan authors he had so carefully built up in Rome.

Cum ieronimus neglectis libris ppheticis i fistent
platonicis tã seua febre corripitur ut uital calor
i suo pretore palpitaret et ante tribunal iudicis
xani se ẽ p fateretur au uidex metuis gratior iani

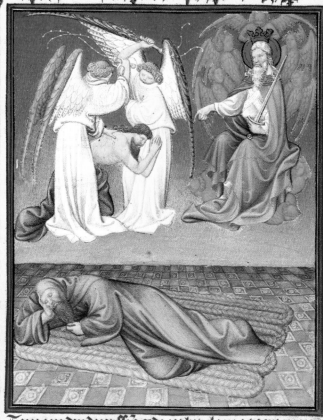

Tunc iudex durissie edi iubet damat ieronimus
domine miseré mei qã sũ hijs libris plus legero
te negalo et statim dimissus reuiuixit lacinus
ptusus et suĩ scapulas tãblès repit acatrices

Fol. 184   St. Jerome ordained as Cardinal.   JEAN OR HERMAN

After that he read the sacred books with as much zeal as he had read pagan books formerly. He achieved such perfection in the Holy Scriptures and in sanctity of life that he was ordained presbyter and cardinal by the Roman Church when he was thirty.

The Pope sits enthroned above his cardinals, who occupy elaborately carved choir stalls on either side. Only two wear the traditional scarlet robes, two are clothed in blue *cappas* as in Paul's Great Litany miniature (73v), and others have placed their hats over white monastic habits. In the foreground two bishops or mitered abbots sit on the ground, formally facing each other like heraldic supporters. Jerome has regained his halo and, facing the Pope, he kneels to receive the cardinal's hat.

Jerome is clothed in monastic brown among these princes of the Church, and in fact he never wished to rise above the rank of presbyter. The medieval world, however, could not believe that the author of the Vulgate held no official position. Of the four great Doctors of the Church Gregory was Pope, Ambrose archbishop, and Augustine a bishop, and therefore long after his death Jerome was conceived to have been a cardinal.

Fol. 184v   St. Jerome in Woman's Dress.   JEAN

On the death of Pope Liberius by common accord Jerome was proclaimed worthy to be supreme pontiff but, shamefully deceived by certain [monks], he [mistakenly] put on a woman's dress instead of his own, and was derided by them at Matins. [Seeing that their] madness was so great, he left this place.

Jerome had many rich Roman ladies among his disciples and not unnaturally these friendships became a subject of gossip. He was an outspoken critic of the laxity of the clergy and monastic communities and, according to the *Golden Legend*, it was a trick they played on him that induced Jerome to leave Rome forever. The subject is rarely represented; we have been able to find only a single and quite unrelated example (Vatican Library, lat. 8541, p. 77).

The miniature relates two successive moments. On the right the saint sleeps peacefully in bed in a colonnaded cloister. A little old monk, mostly muffled, stealthily places a blue dress just where the saint, when he rises still sleepy for Matins, will find it. On the left, carrying a lantern and quite unaware of his grotesque appearance, Jerome joins his brothers for the night Office. Two monks whisper and point at the strange apparition. The chapel with the monks in choir resembles closely, and probably derives from, Paul's miniature for All Soul's Day (221).

Fol. 185 St. Jerome leaves Constantinople.

And he came to Gregory of Nazianzus, Bishop of Constantinople; having studied the sacred books with him, he hastened to the wilderness. Of his sufferings there he has written to Eustochium: My scaly skin was as black as an Ethiopian's.

In this miniature we are shown two successive moments in Jerome's departure from the capital of the Eastern Empire. On the left the saint, identified by his brown habit and solid gold halo, is embraced by Gregory Nazianzus, here remarkably youthful for an eminent theologian. Accompanied by a procession of acolytes carrying a scarlet standard and a holy water situla, the bishop has come to the gates to bid his disciple farewell. On the right the saint, now with a halo of golden rays, is aboard a craft that resembles those on folios 173 and 178v. Great cities appear on the horizon and an imperial galley approaches on a white, green, and gold sea.

Fol. 185v St. Jerome contemplates the Holy Sepulcher.

How often as I dwelt in that waste, in that vast solitude burnt away by the heat of the sun, which provides a terrible abode for monks, I imagined myself among the delights of Rome. My twisted limbs shuddered in a garment of sackcloth.

Although the texts beneath three of these miniatures are from Jerome's famous letter to his pupil Eustochium describing his sufferings in the desert, the entire cycle places greater emphasis on his scholarship and his ecclesiastical career. Here the saint kneels in prayer in a remarkably pallid church. He wears not sackcloth but a monastic habit, and the only reminder—perhaps fortuitous—of extraordinary penances is his hat, not a cardinal's but of brown felt, like those of the flagellants on 74v. The tomb beneath the cupola can only represent the Holy Sepulcher with the sleeping guards. Jerome keeps the Good Friday vigil and shares in spirit the anguish of the apostles.

Fol. 186 St. Jerome tempted by Dancing Girls.

Daily I wept, daily I groaned, and when overcome by sleep I resisted, my bones scarcely holding together were bruised by the ground. Although my only companions were scorpions I often imagined I was surrounded by dancing girls, who kindled the fires of lust.

A devil grasps Jerome's halo and turns his gaze from a church to a mirage conjured up for his torment. The preceding text refers to the delights of Rome, and Jean has placed the two languid young dancers safely within the walls of a city. They are the contemporary equivalents of the young Roman women of Jerome's day. Perhaps the painter, or certainly his adviser, knew his strictures on "gay and thoughtless girls . . . who use cosmetics to improve their skins and affect tight sleeves, dresses without a crease, and dainty buskins; and by pretending to be virgins sell themselves into destruction."

Tanto autem studio libros diuinos ex tuc legit
quito libros gentiliu unqz legerat pfeareqz ilacis
scripturis et scitate uite qz dum eet annor. xxr.
ab ecca romana plbr cardial ordinatus est.

Mortuo aut liberio papa ieronimus dign̄ suūm̄
sacerdocio ab oib3 acclamatur sz derisus tuipit
a quibusdā veste muliebrē p sua induit et ad ma-
tutmū derisus ab eis tācē isanie locum dedit.

Et ad gregorium nazanzenū constātino poli
tane urbēepm uenut a quo pp̄ lacras lr̄as didiat
ad hemū p̄erauit ubi q̄nta sustinuerit ad eusto
chuum sc̄bit. sca hdr artis sigi ethio pracius add.

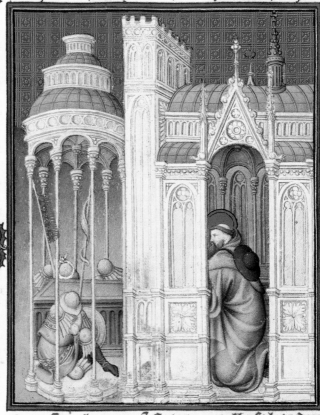

Quicqıes in heremo cōstitutus et illa solitudine
uasta exusta solis ardoribʒ qʒ horridū mona
chis habitaculū prestat putaui me romanıs
intesse deliaꝭ horrebant sacco mēbra deformıa

Quondie lacume quondie gemitus et si quando
repugnate som pn̄ oppliste humo vix ossa herē
cia collidebant er cu scorpio nū tm̄ socuis sepr cho
ris puellaru mỉesse ⁊ sola libidinū mcendia

Quadã die leo claudicãs monasteriũ igressus
est ieronim' aut cum ceti fugent qui hospiti obui
at leo pede oñdit q̃z adhibita cura diligenti
libiatur et oi securate ãposita inter eos habitat

One day a lion came limping into the monastery. Those who were with Jerome fled, but he went to meet it and the lion held out its paw. Healed by devoted attention and losing all ferocity it lived among them.

According to the *Golden Legend* it was in Bethlehem, where Jerome established himself with a group of monks after his years in the desert, that a lion entered the monastery at the hour of evening prayer. In the miniature, however, the painter has placed the scene, like so many others in the manuscript, outside a high arched entrance and beside the most elaborate of the stone fountains that are a feature of the miniatures illustrating the eremitical life (191, 192v, 193v, 194). The monks who had scattered in terror have ventured back to watch the saint's ministrations, though only the young brother who holds the jar and towel seems completely reassured. Jerome, his book laid aside, touches the wound and eyes the lion, which opens its mouth for an answering roar.

Tradition has made the lion Jerome's inseparable companion, but the legend of the beast who in gratitude for the removal of a thorn faithfully served a community of monks originated with Gerasimus, a lesser-known abbot from farther up the Jordan.

The miniature is exceptional for its fine brushwork, especially in the rendering of the fluid folds of the soft, creamy, brown habits of Jerome and his disciples.

Another day the lion, overcome by drowsiness while guarding the ass, fell asleep. He awoke, and not finding his companion sought him here and there, roaring. Seeing the ass coming from afar together with some camels, he compelled them to flee toward the monastery.

Since Jerome believed the lion had been sent by providence to serve the monks he proposed that the animal be used to guard the donkey, which had been assigned the task of carrying firewood.

In the middle distance the lion sleeps peacefully, unaware that his charge, grazing nearby, is about to be captured by a passing train of merchants. The return of the lion alone to the monastery is not represented but in the background we do see the punishment inflicted on him by the saint, because all were convinced that he had killed and eaten the ass. The lion is now reduced to a beast of burden, and a lay-brother places on his back wood cut by a companion.

The short text below the miniature is based as usual on the *Golden Legend*, which tells more fully the story represented in the foreground of the miniature. The lion, freed after his day's work, had caught sight of a passing caravan of merchants with camels, led in the manner of the country by an ass. Recognizing his lost companion, he bounded after them and drove the entire party to the monastery gates, as we see. The painter has, however, departed from the *Golden Legend* in showing the lion, followed by a woodcutter, scattering firewood as he leaps forward to exonerate himself. Two merchants look back in terror, while another, quite diminutive before the towering saint, begs forgiveness. The source of the trouble, the ass, is only partly visible, and a camel grazes quietly at Jerome's feet.

We can be certain that the painters had living models nearby for the exotic animals in this animated miniature. Since the lion was the emblem of Burgundy their first patron, Philippe le Hardi, kept one or more of them in his entourage. We know that Jean de Berry possessed a camel, tended by a special keeper.

Alia aut̃ uice aͧſtodieſ aſinũ leo ſompnˀ gͣat̃
dozmiuiͭ aſinũ pdͥt exhͥgͤ tͧiſ uigileſ ſociũ
nõ repeͥt hͫc ĩ de ǵt aſinũ a longe uͤnienͭͤ
uidet cū camellˀ quoſ ad mõ ſteriũ fugͤ coegit.

Per quadrienniũ igitur iero?. in hiero pña pac
ta ut pruoẽs aıal ao psepe oñı bethlee remeauıt
ubı arca trñslacioñe bıblıe aclacrarũ scrıptãrz
lr̃. ãnıs et vj. menlıbʒ oeluoauıt ıugo p̃maneʃ

Having, therefore, done penance in the wilderness for four years, Jerome went to dwell like a domestic animal at the manger of the Lord in Bethlehem where, remaining chaste, he labored for fifty-five years and six months at the translation of the Bible and the Holy Scriptures.

This miniature of the saint in his study reflects a cult of Jerome as a scholar that was promoted in the first half of the fourteenth century by Johannes Andreae, a professor of canon law in Bologna. Soon thereafter painters in North Italy began to produce images of Jerome in a well-stocked study, and French representations of this type, though simpler than their Italian counterparts, appeared in the circle of Charles V. Records of the collections of this learned King describe a splendid enamel, or *joyau*, of Jerome between a lectern and a lion. The Bolognese lawyer recommended that Jerome should be represented as a cardinal, and in these paintings of the saint in his study he usually has at least the distinctive large, red hat.

Here, however, Jerome is a simple tonsured monk, although with a double halo—a golden disk combined with rays. The pews for his disciples remain curiously empty. Only his loyal and ever-grateful lion accompanies the saint. Three of the sixteen prophets whose books he translated appear waving blank scrolls on a battlemented terrace surrounding an upper story. Strangely—and this is unique in the book—they are not statues but people of flesh and blood, as much alive as Jerome himself. Prophets or saints appear on other buildings (30, 96, 184v, 189v), but they are always statues of stone, part of the architectural structure. The idea of animating these Old Testament personages seems most consonant with Herman's art, and we probably see his hand in their features and demonstrative gestures.

Statues as part of the architecture may be seen again in the famous drawing of St. Jerome in his study in the *Bible moralisée* in Paris. That drawing is based in our opinion on a lost composition by the Limbourgs of about 1411, which resembled in many respects this miniature in the *Belles Heures*.

This famous man, reaching the end of his days and fortified by the Sacrament, sank down stretched out on the ground, placing his hands in the form of the cross on his breast. Suddenly his soul departed and, like a star resplendent with all the virtues, entered Heaven.

Jerome died in the year 420 in his monastery of Bethlehem. The *Golden Legend* does not describe his death and burial and therefore the texts beneath the last miniatures of the cycle are drawn from two apocryphal letters, supposedly by Eusebius of Cremona and St. Augustine. The letters were widely disseminated and they could have been found in a copy of *The Lives of the Fathers* which, in a French translation, appeared in the 1402 inventory of the Duke's library.

The saint, stripped of his monastic habit and wearing only the hair shirt of a hermit, has chosen to die outside on the stony ground, his head resting on a rock. The sorrowing monks have gathered within the entrance to their church to recite the prayers for the dying. Members of the neighboring communities, or perhaps venerable hermits to judge from their ample beards, have assembled at the news. One head extends over the gold frame of the miniature, giving the impression of a still greater, unseen throng. Most of those present have their eyes fixed on the dying saint, who despite his great age (eighty-eight according to the *Golden Legend*) has a thick brown beard. Matted locks have replaced the tonsure of preceding miniatures. Only one or two young brothers look up toward the luminous Deity, who awaits the supernatural ascent of the saint's small, naked soul, borne in a sling by angels arrayed in palest yellow, violet, and rose.

The entire scene around Jerome's mortal remains is rendered in shades of brown, ranging from the buff of the stone portal and the bloodless limbs of the corpse to the golden tones of the habits and the orange-brown desert peak. The painter has carefully differentiated the features of the monks and hermits, and he described with a similar penetrating realism the limbs of the saint and the toes flexed in the rigidity of death. Is not Paul's influence discernible in this miniature?

Hic uir gloriosus ad extremum uite ductus sup
to sacramento supinus ad tram redyt manus
i modu auas sup pectus tenes et statim aia san
cuma ut sydo oibz iuuarubz radias celos adyt.

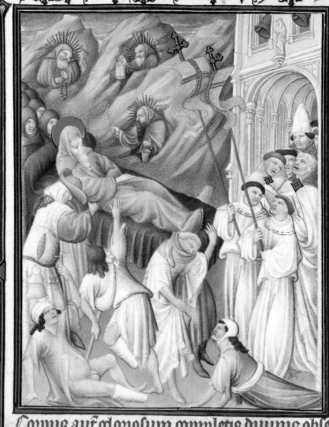

Corpus aut̃ gloriosum completis diuinis oble
quijs ad bethlee̅ uix p̃sepe dn̅i coopertum tm̅
lintheo sacco in terra sepelitur q̅ntas aut̃ miracul
dn̅s eu̅ mirificauit lingua no̅ sufficit enarrare

When the holy obsequies were over the glorious body, enveloped only in a hair tunic, was buried in the earth at Bethlehem, near the manger of the Lord. No tongue can name the number of miracles with which God honored him.

In this very complex composition Jean has combined around the saint's mortal remains four different events. In the background holy hermits emerge from their caves; one holds a lantern, another tells his beads, and a third scatters blessed water as the bier passes, followed by Jerome's monks with covered heads. According to the apocryphal letter on which the title here is based Bishop Cyril came from Jerusalem to conduct the funeral, and in the miniature he emerges from the church, towering in his miter above the procession. Acolytes bear waving banners, bells toll, and officiating clergy in cream copes over white surplices chant from a rose-covered book.

In the foreground maimed and sick struggle to approach the bier. An averted youth missing a foot leans on his stick and stretches up his hand to touch the corpse. Across the path of the pallbearers a beggar in a tattered garment of pearly green lies stretched, partly beyond the frame. Most striking is the cripple who leans back supporting his weight on his stick and on his right hand. His farther leg is bent while the nearer one, lacking a foot, is stretched before him. This figure, anticipated by Jean Pucelle nearly a century earlier in a manuscript belonging to the Duke, caught the attention of French illuminators of the early fifteenth century, who introduced it into various subjects. Whereas in their miniatures in the *Bible moralisée* the Limbourgs allowed only devils to display their genitals, Jean has extended his realism in this respect to the half-naked cripple.

The painter has not been entirely successful in placing the bier firmly on the shoulders of the bearers. At first sight it might seem to rest on higher ground, while the man with a yellow hood and his companion with a broad-brimmed hat and pink purse at his belt gesture somewhat aimlessly. Further inspection shows that the rose hat on the far side belongs to the blue-skirted bearer at the foot of the bier, and of the man at the head a peach skirt is visible. When depicting the same person in successive scenes painters sometimes varied his features, and Jerome, who on the recto preserved his dark hair in death, has here, perhaps as the center of a cult, a long white beard.

During the persecution of Decius St. Paul, the first hermit, fled from Rome after he had seen a Christian, who was bound in a place of delights and caressed by a lewd woman, bite off his tongue and spit it in her face, so that the pain put to flight the temptation.

The decision of the painters or of their advisers to add to the life of St. Jerome a similar series of miniatures on Sts. Paul and Anthony was probably influenced by the fact that the account of the two desert Fathers in the *Golden Legend* was based, as it states, on Jerome's *Life of Paul the First Hermit*.

The cycle begins with the scene of a young Christian subjected to a torment so horrifying to Paul that he decides to abandon the world and flee to the desert. In a secluded, leafy garden a richly dressed youth lies pinioned, his arms behind him, caressed by a young woman described in the contemporary French translation of the *Golden Legend* as "surpassingly beautiful of body but unchaste." In keeping with her profession she wears a close-fitting dress with a low decolletage, and her hair is dressed in the fashionable *cornettes* denounced as frivolous by contemporary Parisian preachers. To illustrate the "murmuring waters" of the idyllic setting described by the *Golden Legend* Jean, who painted much of this cycle, has placed the scene near a monumental stone fountain. The young man, about to be overcome by pleasure, bites off his tongue in desperation and spits it into the bland, expressionless face of the temptress.

At the upper right Paul raises a hand and averts his eyes in horror. Behind him a tall, stern man watches the couple intently. He is younger than Paul and although he is in brown he cannot be a hermit because a decorative band is visible around his neck. Perhaps he is meant for Anthony, who followed Paul into the wilderness some years later.

In this miniature, as in the greater part of the cycle, heavy, saturated tones predominate. Although in the book this series follows the life of St. Jerome it might have been painted earlier, before Jean had decided to emulate Paul's delicate, luminous palette.

Sanctꝰ paulꝰ p̓mꝰ he̅mita feruēte p̓ſecuc̅o̅e de
ai̅uſo q̓ xp̓ianus q̓ui̅di̅ mͤ ame̅na ligat̓ et
ab ip̓ndica ti̅tat̓ linguā abſadit et mͤi̅ facie̅ꝯ
ſpuit ut tempta c̅o̅ne do̅lor̅ fuga ꝯet. roma fug̅

Fol. 191v   St. Anthony seeking St. Paul's Hermitage.

Terrified by this and by other penalties, Paul fled from Rome and crossed the ocean. He reached a vast desert beside the Red Sea. Later Anthony learned in a dream of one better than himself dwelling in the wilderness.

Unaware that after forty years of solitude he is soon to have company, Paul sits outside his hermitage bent over a book. The water of the Red Sea is, as in some other paintings of this time, given the full color suggested by its name, whereas the pond nearby is a beautiful limpid blue. To create the impression of vastness the painter has carried the landscape right up to the top of the frame, but it seems to rise as much as to recede. The colors grow deeper, and the oared galley is painted almost as distinctly as the hissing reptile in Anthony's path. The robust figure of the saint was no doubt designed, and perhaps painted, by Paul. He strides forward energetically, his cloak thrown carelessly over a shoulder, holding his staff jauntily rather than, as Jerome says, "to support the weak limbs of a venerable old man." It is important to the story that the two hermits should be clearly distinguished and Anthony therefore retains his brown hair and beard until his death.

Fol. 192   St. Anthony directed by a Centaur.

And while he [Anthony] was searching through the forests [he met] a centaur, who pointed the way with his right hand. Then he came across a satyr, a god of the forests according to the error of the pagans, and finally a wolf who led him to Paul's cell.

"Of all the pilgrim routes a man may follow overseas none is so lonely or so strange as the way from St. Anthony's abbey to St. Paul's." So wrote Ogier d'Anglure, a French pilgrim in 1398, and in such surroundings he, like Jerome before him, was quite prepared to accept the reality of a centaur or satyr. Here the saint is confronted by a combination of both: the torso of a man with the four legs of a centaur but the cleft hoofs and goat-hair proper to a satyr. The powerful hermit of the facing miniature has been transformed by the painter (probably Jean) into a dignified abbot with carefully combed hair and a silky beard, wearing a habit of dark brown that falls in graceful folds and spreads about his feet. The brutish creature imitates Anthony's benediction as he points to Paul sitting by a stone sarcophagus, amid barren hills inhabited by a lion and a giant millipede. A small pool of blue water lies on Anthony's way and here an animal of the Duke's menagerie, the giraffe, comes to drink.

Having met they fell into each other's arms. Indeed, at mealtime a raven brought a double ration of bread. A pious dispute arose between them [as to] who should first divide the bread. Paul offered it to [his] guest, Anthony to [his] senior. [Finally] both took hold of it.

The miniature departs from the text and indeed from the traditional iconography for the miraculous feeding of the two saints. From a disk of blue sky the Holy Ghost himself descends as a dove, bearing a communion wafer marked with a cross. A Sienese panel of about 1400, now in Berlin, shows a raven with spread wings bringing a Host to the kneeling hermits, but the Limbourgs were the first to transform the *corvus* into a white dove. Anthony, shading his eyes from the heavenly radiance, looks up in astonishment, while Paul, for whom this is a daily occurrence, calmly turns a page.

The two hermits are differentiated by the color of their hair—Paul is the elder— as well as by their haloes and the shades of brown in their habits. Anthony's billowing mantle is superbly modulated in small strokes of dark pigment laid with a very fine brush, and the miniature in general has the high finish of Jean's best work. According to the Breviary the Fathers took their evening repast by a fountain, at the hour when "young lions roar after their prey and seek their meat from God." Here a giraffe and lion prance with open mouths and a large green dragon emerges from a cave.

Fol. 193   St. Paul's Soul transported by Angels.   JEAN

But when Anthony was returning through the desert he saw angels bearing Paul's soul and hastening back he found Paul's corpse erect with knees bent as if in prayer. O holy soul, he said, what you did in life you still show in death.

In one of the distant hermitages Paul, although dead, still kneels in prayer, in accordance with the title of the miniature. Anthony has been halted by the vision of angels flying up with the soul of his friend through the only blue sky in this entire cycle. In astonishment the saint has dropped his cane, bell, and book, and his outstretched hand directs our attention to the small, youthful kneeling figure tenderly supported by the celestial messengers. Their long floating draperies and the ends of the sling flutter like the pennons of the departing ship on the Red Sea beneath. The landscape in these two facing miniatures is very differently designed from the wilderness on 191v and 192, where it rises as much as it recedes. Here Jean has clearly distinguished — also in color—the foreground, the middleground, and the far, bleached hills surrounding the Red Sea.

Huius ante et aliorū pēius paul⁹ pīcturus wo
ma fugiēs maria trāsuit ⁊ uastissimā herēmū
pēijt secus mare rubrum p⁹ quod tēpꝰ āthonī
meltore̅ e̅ se heremū incolere edocetur ī sompnio

Quē dum p ſiluas anthoni⁹ quereret ypotē
taurū obuiā ht qui ei⁹ dexta uiā ad paulū de
mōſtrat ide ſatirū rept ſiluax dei errore gētiliū
et tandē lupū q̃ eum ad pauli cellam adduxit.

Quo repto ambo in āplexū nuir adestq̄ cornuus
duplicatā panis alterꝰ parte hoia prandij. Int̄
pꝝs pia lis oꝛit q̄s ꝑmo panē diuidat deferr paulꝰ
hoſpiti antoniuis ſciōn utꝗ̄ manū apponit.

Cum aut anthoni' redurt pdferta uidit angelos
aiam pauli deferetes q uelodt redies fueut corp
pauli flexis genibz in modu orantis erectu mirat
qz dixit o sca aia qd in uita gebas i morte mo stra'u

Cum auit nõ heret unde sepelurt aduenere leo
nes duo et boueã puãt sepltoq̃ ad siluã redeũt
ãthoni' auc tunicã ꝑ ex palmis et terciã assũp sic
q̃ i solenibus utebat̃ ãno dñi ij° lxxx septimo.

And as he had nothing [with which] to bury him, there came two lions who made ready
the grave and then returned to the forest. Anthony took Paul's tunic made of palm leaves
and wore it on high feast days. [He died] in the year 287.

Two preceding scenes included a handsome sarcophagus but Paul had specifically re-
quested to be laid in the ground. Since no hermit ever tilled the earth Anthony found
himself without a spade. So far the beasts of the desert have gone quietly about their
business, but here, as the title states, two lions come and start to do what lions never
do in nature—dig. According to Jerome "they were roaring aloud as if to make known
that they were mourning in the only way possible to them," and since it is difficult to
dig and roar simultaneously Jean has added a third, who casts his eyes prayerfully to
heaven.

In life St. Paul was tonsured and attired in a monastic habit, but now his hair
hangs in long tresses and he goes into the grave in the tunic of palm leaves he is said to
have plaited himself. The painter has thus departed from the title, which clearly says
that Anthony took this tunic for his own use. Anthony's ruddy complexion contrasts
with the pallor of the corpse, a pallor that is accentuated by contrast with the rich
brown earth and the tawny lions. The lions, in turn, are matched exactly by the tunic
of palm leaves. A small pool of blue water catches the light and brightens the right
corner near the kneeling saint, who has laid his staff and platter beside it. The compact
triangle of the burial party and of a green hermitage lying diagonally across the
composition is balanced by the tall, violet fountain and the pink vertical of a building
that rises above a craggy peak where a dragon has made his home.

Once, when this glorious saint had taken refuge in a tomb, a multitude of devils set about him, lacerating him in such a way that his companion, taking him for dead, carried him away on his shoulders. Afterwards, while they were all asleep, he suddenly revived.

The last two miniatures in the cycle have titles from the account of Anthony in the *Golden Legend*, based this time on the life of the saint by Athanasius rather than Jerome. It speaks of the Desert Fathers inhabiting Egyptian tombs. Such rock-hewn caverns were unknown in the North and, like the painter of a somewhat earlier Lombard miniature,[9] Jean shows the saint lying in a fine arcaded sarcophagus, placed diagonally and closely resembling Christ's tomb in 152v.

With his large head and strong, expressive features Anthony now resembles the robust man who set out on 191v to seek Paul the Hermit. The devils have taken precisely the forms of those beasts which in earlier miniatures were friendly or even helpful to the hermits. A sinuous reptile slithers over the side and under the folds of the saint's brown habit; a lion attacks him from behind and gnaws at his shoulder, and a snake-headed dragon fastens its sharp white fangs in his beard. He is helpless to fend them off because the devil in his own shape has grasped his arm and bites into his wrist as he raises his cudgel to belabor the saint. The craggy peak rising above him adds to the devil's power. A tall blue fountain and the pink of a small hermitage at the upper right direct the eye to the conventional red and blue dragon of the border and seem to involve it in the scene.

A small, gold-colored porringer lies prominently in the foreground beside the pool. Together with Anthony's crutch it was present in the preceding miniature. Here, however, it may refer to another occasion. The Latin text of the *Golden Legend* says the devil placed in Anthony's path a golden *discus*, which was translated in the contemporary French version as *escuelle* or small dish. The saint passed it by and the porringer vanished in a puff of smoke.

Hic sanctꝰ gloriosus dūi quedā tumulo lati
tant adest multitudo demonū q̄ eū talit̃ laca
uit q̄ eꝰ munist̃ eū q̄ mortuū sup humos ad
portauit ꝑea dormientibus cũctis sbīto reuiuix

Tandē beatus āthonius ꝑ multa ⁊ inumerabilia
demonum temptamēta q̄ passus ē duī uita
heremitica ducēt quā scē ⁊ plenū a xr̄ sue uite an̄
no uſq; ad. C.v. quieuit ī pace āno dn̄i. iij. xl.

Fol. 194v   The Death of St. Anthony.

At last the blessed Anthony, after many and innumerable temptations of the devil endured during his life as a hermit, which he lived from his twentieth to his hundred and fifth year, fell asleep in the year of the Lord 340.

Anthony the hermit is generally known as St. Anthony Abbot, although he fled from the community which gathered around him and chose to end his life in the solitude of a rock-hewn tomb. He took precautions, according to Athanasius, to avoid a devotion to his remains, but references to these as well as to the manner of his burial were omitted both from the *Golden Legend* and from the Breviary. Later centuries, in any event, invoked him against the scourge of ergotism, known as St. Anthony's Fire, and kings and princes visited his relics at Vienne, the mother house of the Antonines, the oldest Order of Hospitalers.

The dead saint lies in a vaulted chamber seen, like most interiors in the manuscript, through arches supported by a central column. Unlike Diocrès on 94v he has not been given a coffin covered with a pall but lies on bare boards supported by trestles. There are no tall candlesticks; the room is lit by plain oil lamps in wall brackets, and light enters through windows that disclose a bright blue sky. The Last Rites are of an austerity suitable to hermits living in community, and the painter probably had in mind the simple ceremonies of a cenobitical Order such as the Carthusians.

Fire burns in an earthenware jar, perhaps to purify the air, and a situla and aspergillum for sprinkling holy water stand on the tesselated floor. The rather bright tiles and the deep blue vaults contrast with the brown of the four holy monks. The painter gave each of the books from which they read the Office a delicious color, marvelously chosen to enrich a somber scene.

We meet here the new way of representing this central Christian event. It has assumed a form that had appeared in Italian painting in the late fourteenth century, under the influence of the *Meditations on the Life of Christ* and the *Revelations of St. Bridget* (ca. 1370). In it the Virgin no longer lies in bed alongside the infant's crib; she as well as Joseph adore the newborn Child who lies on the ground between them.

This new adoration of the Child was first introduced into France in the Duke's earlier *Très Belles Heures de Notre-Dame.* Paul adopted it, together with a reference to the cave described by St. Bridget, in a miniature in the *Bible moralisée.* The painter expanded the theme by adding shepherds, in whom he had, as we have seen, a special interest. In the *Belles Heures* two of them, standing in a defile, hail the event while two others on the hills receive the news from heaven. In Paul's earlier miniature, too, the Virgin prays in her white tunic, Joseph raises a hand in surprise as well as veneration, and rays issue from God the Father and from the infant.

In the *Belles Heures* the rays have become much more prominent than in the *Bible*; they anticipate the scintillating shower of light in the *Nativity* in the *Très Riches Heures.* In that later composition Paul gave still more prominence to the shepherds. Although the *Nativity* on the facing plate is artistically weaker than the one in the *Très Riches Heures* and by Jean rather than Paul, it anticipates that miniature in several respects—certainly more than does the *Nativity* in the Hours of the Virgin (48v). This similarity is one more sign of the comparatively late date, during the work on the *Belles Heures,* of the execution of the illustrations of the suffrages and the Masses.

rabilia fect. Puer natus.

Gloria pri. Puer natus.

kyriel. kyriel. kyriel.

xpel. xpel. xpeleison.

kyriel. kyriel. kyriel.

Gloria in excelsis

deo. Et in terra

pax hominib; bone volu

tatis. Laudamus te. Bn

dicimus te. Adoramus

te. Glorificamus te. Gra

cias agimus tibi propter

magnam gloriam tua.

Domine deus rex celestis.

deus pater omnipotens.

Domine fili unigenite

ihu xpe. Domine deus a

agnus dei filius pris. Qui

tollis pctã mundi mise

rere nobis. Qui tollis

pctata mundi suscipe

De natiuitate dni ãc.

Puer natus

est nobis t

filius datu'

est nobis cuius imperiu

super humerum eius et

uocabitur nomen mag

consily angelus ps.

Cantate domino can

ticum nouum: quia mi

Fol. 198   The Resurrection. *Easter Sunday Mass.*

Books of Hours of the fourteenth and early fifteenth century place a greater emphasis on the sufferings and death of Christ than on his miraculous resurrection. The Hours of the Passion, which most of them contain, usually end with the entombment or, as in this book, with the guards watching at the tomb (152v). The decision to include in the *Belles Heures*, however, a series of Masses for the principal feasts of the liturgical year gave this scene, so central to the Christian faith, at least a place.

The painting resembles closely Herman's last miniature of the Hours of the Passion showing the closed tomb (152v). The setting is similar—a conical peak facing the walled city of Jerusalem on a hillside. The three sleeping guards are dressed in similar colors, and one of them again holds a shield in the form of a grotesque mask. The sarcophagus, too, is arcaded and placed diagonally to the picture plane. Perhaps to suggest the early hour the sky is streaked and the peak capped by clouds.

In miniatures by Pucelle and other forerunners of the Limbourgs Christ often emerges from the tomb a calm, frontal, awesome person. Already in the *Bible moralisée* of 1402–1404, however, the Limbourgs had shown him stepping out of the tomb, holding a cross-staff and looking back. Here he wears an unusual violet cloak held by a large golden clasp. Blood marks the wounds in his hands and side, and a pennon, scarlet like the *oriflamme* that the French kings carried into battle, flutters from his staff. His departure is informal and hastened, it seems, by the flying angel toward whom he turns his head.

Gnus dei qui tollis
peccata mundi dona no
bis pacem. Communio.
Viderunt omnes fines
terre salutare dei nostri. Et
Presta precom.
Quesumus
omnipotens deus:
ut natus hodie salua
tor mundi sicut diui
ne nobis generacio
nis est auctor: ita et
immortalitatis sit ipse
largitor. Per diim.
nim ihesum xpm fi
lium tuum qui tecii
uiuit et regnat in u
nitate eiusdem spiritus
sancti deus per omnia
secula seculorum. Amen.
In die pasche. Introit.

Esurrexi et
adhuc tecii
sum alla.
posuisti sup me manii
tuam alla mirabilis fa
est sciencia tua alla. pf.
Domine probasti me
et cognouisti me: tu cog
uisti sessionem meam et
resurrectionem meam.

The descent of the Holy Spirit at Pentecost is the subject of two miniatures earlier in the manuscript (84, 155). For the feast itself the painter or his adviser therefore decided to represent the continued presence of the third person of the Trinity in the celebration of the Eucharist.

With only a single, rather simple but pious man as server, the priest conducts what seems a rather unfestive Mass for so important a feast. The violet altar, covered by a white cloth, is devoid of ornament. There is no painted altarpiece or figurative relief, and the high stone reredos is decorated only with arcading and a panel carved with acanthus leaves. The celebrant bows low as he prepares to break the Host over the golden chalice before taking Communion. On the altar lies the purificator, a white linen cloth folded in three, which the priest will use to wipe the chalice after the ablutions. Above, the Holy Ghost in the form of a dove hovers unseen by the celebrant or his server.

The figure of the priest was surely inspired by Bruno on 97. His buff mantle is almost as delicate and luminous as Bruno's white. The billowing folds and gliding movement have, indeed, much of the beauty of their magnificent model.

tem omnia prospiciens.
Spiritus domini. V.
Gloria pri. Spus do.
kyriel. iij. xpel. iij.
kyrieleison. iij.
Gloria in excelsis.
Deus qui oro
hodierna die
corda fidelium sancti
spiritus illustracione
docuisti: da nobis in
eodem spiritu recta sa
pere: et de eius semp
sancta consolacione
gaudere. Per in uni
tate eiusdem. Lectio
actuum aplor
diebus illis:
dum comple
rentur dies penthe co
stes: erant omnes di

Spiritus
domini
replevit
orbem terrarum allelu
ia. et hoc quod continet
omnia scienciam habet
nocis alleluya alleluya
alleluya. psalmus dd.
Omnium est enim ar
tifex omnem hns virtu

God the Father holds in his outstretched arms the crucified Christ, who is much smaller in scale, while the Holy Ghost hovers between them. The representation of the Trinity in this form is an invention of the twelfth century; however the usual designation, Throne of Grace, is a translation of *Gnadenstühl*, a term first used by Luther in the sixteenth century.

The Father, seated on the clouds in the firmament of heaven, is a majestic figure. His halo, again painted to simulate tooling, is proportionately the largest in the book, and it is made still more impressive by the encircling scarlet cherubim.

All the strong colors—the fiery cherubim, the gold arabesque, and the blue clouds —lie outside the figures. The Trinity itself has a soft, pale unity of hue. The Father's violet mantle falls loosely across his lap and spreads out on the clouds that form his footstool. His eyes are turned to the left, and Christ's bowed head and flexed knees as well as the Holy Ghost move in the same direction. The painter has reestablished a balance by raising the crossbar at the right and by exposing on that side more of the white of the Father's tunic.

sco loquentes magna
lia dei alleluya allelu
ya. post comunione
Sancti spiritus
Donc corda nfa
mundet infusio et
sui roris intima asp
sione fecundet. per
dominum nfm ihe
sum xpm filium tuu
qui tecum uuut et re
gnat in unitate ciuf
dem spiritus sancti ds
per omnia secula se
culorum. Amen.
Benedicamus do
mino.
Deo gracias.
Of illa de sancta tri
nitate.

Benedicta
sit sancta
trinitas
atq, indiuisa unitas
confitebimur ei quia
fecit nobiscum mism
suam. psalmus
Benedicamus patm
et filium cum sco spu
laudemus et super exal

Fol. 209   Madonna and two Angels. *Mass of the Madonna.*   PAUL

In this small miniature Paul effortlessly suspends a voluminous Madonna and Child high in the space. The curling arabesques serve to sustain them, while the golden sun and diverging rays below supply a counterforce. The weight of the majestic Madonna and the robust Child are carried, too, by the flow of drapery and by the conformity of the rectangular pattern of figures with the upper rectangle of the frame.

In this little masterpiece the painter has employed a favorite range of color—rose, buff, white, green, and blue. The power and mode of Paul's vision bring to mind Masaccio.

gnus dei qui tollis.
gnus dei qui tollis.
gnus dei qui tollis.

er ligniū sei com̄-
ūi facti sūmus et persciam
quarm̄ tita liberati sumu
fuerit. auctous seducit no
filius dei redēit nos al
leluia. secunda oratio.

Esto nobis
dom̄ine deus
nr̄. et quos sancte eu-
ꝰis letari facis honore
eius q̄ paꝗ perpetuis
deffende subsidiis. P
dominum nostrum
Ih̄m filium tuum q̄
tecum uiuit et regn̄. in
unitate eiusdem sp̄us
sc̄i deus per oīa se. se. X.
missa de nr̄a domina

Alue sancta
parens enica
puerpera regē
qui celum terram q̄ regit
in secula seculorum. ps.
Post partum uirgo
inuiolata pmansisti dei
genitrix intercede pro nob.
Salue sc̄a parens. X.
Gloria pri et filio 7 sp.

Fleeing the city crowds, he sought the desert caves in his tender years. A camel provided the rough covering for his holy limbs, [the skin] of a sheep his girdle. His drink [was] of water, his food honey together with locusts. Other seers with prophetic spirit sang of the shining light that was to come. [Text ends on 211v.]

The titles beneath the first two miniatures celebrating the Duke's name saint are taken from a hymn for Matins of the Nativity of the Baptist. The short cycle begins with an enigmatic and apparently unprecedented representation. A monumental and commanding Baptist stands in an uncommonly green and fertile desert. Wrapped in a supple camel skin of a beautiful golden brown reversing to red, he leans to the left while rolling his eyes to the right and striking a rhetorical pose, as if the voice crying in the wilderness were addressing an unseen multitude.

John is flanked by two very different figures, neither of whom can be securely identified from traditional iconography. Both have their eyes fixed on the Lamb, the symbol of Christ. The grave, bearded man on the left must belong to a later time, since he is tonsured and wears a monastic habit. He has no halo but not all saints in the book are given them. Since the Baptist was the model of anchorites could this be St. Anthony Abbot? The Limbourgs, however, invariably dress hermits in brown. Is he perhaps Benedict? Inspired by the Baptist's example the Father of Western Monasticism dedicated to him his first church, and although he normally wears black Benedict is sometimes dressed in bright blue.

The title here may provide a clue to the other enigmatic figure. Could this man, with his uncovered, long, wavy hair and his rose cloak draped around him like a toga, be one of those "other seers" who prophesied the incarnation? *Vates* is a classical Latin word not normally applied to Old Testament prophets, who moreover look very different where they appear in other miniatures of the book (30, 99, 187v). We suggest that this is Virgil, whose famous words in the *Fourth Eclogue* were generally understood to foretell the Incarnation.[10] Here he seems to be counting, leaving free what may be an index finger, as though the Baptist's identification of the Savior with this finger, described in the next title, were transferred to Virgil.[11]

The bears, boars, and a lion in the background may simply denote a wilderness. Boars might, if understood as pigs, refer to St. Anthony. Bears were among the Duke's favorite emblems, and since the title mentions honey the painter possibly thought that one of the animals should search for it up a tree. In the *Temptation* in the *Très Riches Heures*, however, a lion, with other connotations, seems to tree a bear.

Antra deserti teneris sub annis ciuium turmas fugiens pe=
tijt prebuit yrtu tegimē camelus artub; sacris
tuo pleum bidentes cui later austum sociata pōtū
mella locustis cētū trn œcāne uatū corde plago iu

bar ad futurū tu quidē mundo ſcelus auferente
indice prodis non fuit uaſti ḣꝛꝯau̅ pꝛorb ſancti
oꝛ quiſq̄m genitus iohanne qui nephas ſedi
meruit lauantem tingere lymphis.

Thou, however, hast revealed with thy index finger him who bears the sins of the world. Throughout the wide spaces of the universe none was born holier than John, who was found worthy to wash away with water the sins of the world.

Paul's largeness of conception and perfect control of color are nowhere more manifest than in this miniature, with its masterful simplicity and its harmony of tan, gold, pale green, violet, and blue. He has introduced new pictorial qualities, such as the filmy loincloth and the equally transparent water that spills over Christ's head and body, ending finally in the marvelously limpid blue of the pond in which he stands.

The painter has not represented the Jordan as a river, and the miniature is unusual in other respects, also. The Baptist holds a situla, which suggests an association between the water he pours from a scoop—oddly with his left hand—and the baptismal water mixed with oil and chrism blessed annually on Holy Saturday. Christ bends humbly forward with hands crossed on his breast, a position that, though popular later, is rare in contemporary painting.

One unusual aspect—the omission of the Holy Ghost—the miniature shares with the *Baptism* in the Duke's *Très Belles Heures de Notre Dame,* painted shortly before. Since tl.e Trinity was first revealed on this occasion artists usually represented it except when space was limited above. Here Paul had ample room, but he preferred to preserve without interruption the mosaic of red, blue, and gold which extends from the fiery cherubim to the bowed head of the Son. He stressed, however, the unity of the Godhead, giving the Father the Son's gesture of crossed hands. He also dressed him in a robe of violet, a shade deeper than Christ's seamless garment, which is so beautifully displayed by the angel.

Fol. 212   St. John the Baptist beheaded.

Herod, exposed as one blinded by excess, imprisoned John the Baptist. Rashly he gave a promise to the dancing maiden; his crime he excused by his oath. The adulteress felt no horror [at seeing] the head of John—a holy sight—in the hands of her daughter, among the revels of the guests.

John the Baptist reproached Herod for his marriage to his sister-in-law Herodias, whose husband, Philip, was still living. He thus incurred the hatred of Herodias and was cast into prison. At the King's birthday feast Salome, the daughter of Herodias by Philip, so pleased Herod by her dancing that he promised to give her anything she wished. At her mother's prompting she asked for the head of the Baptist on a charger.

Here the executioner with a two-handed blow severs the head of the saint as he leans out of his prison. Perhaps this posture of St. John was, as has been suggested, influenced by early miracle plays, in which a stuffed torso was thrust out of an aperture and the false head struck off.

Salome stands waiting, her veil clasped by a high diadem and her skirt lined with royal ermine. Often she has a bowl, but here she holds a platter of impressive size with a wide, flat edge. She has gathered up her skirt and sways gracefully away from the gruesome sight. The execution is watched by an official and two companions, one of whom puts a hand on his shoulder and looks curiously at the scene—remarkably like a figure in Ambrogio Lorenzetti's fresco in S. Francesco, Siena. The official, like the officer on 157, wears a high, fur busby. He holds a very large, twisted candle as a reminder that fire and light (and later fireworks) are associated with midsummer night, the birthday of John, who came to bear witness "to the true Light" (John 1:9).

Smoke rises from the chimney of the banqueting hall, where Herod and his guests await the return of Salome with the head.

Herodes luxurie cecitate convictus. io. bap. incarcerat
saltanti puelle temere iurat scelus iuramento
excusat matris lacinia con nundaui adulta cap iohis
pium spectaculum i manu filie non horruit.

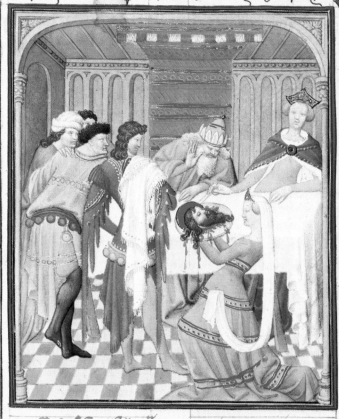

ex illa de sco iohe bap.   cauit me dominus no

...iucunt   ...mine meo et posuit os

...uicnuc ma   ...mcū ut gladuū acutū

...ris mec uo   ...sub tegumento manus

Although this miniature and the preceding one represent the martyrdom of the saint the Mass, which starts here, is not for the Decollation (August 29th) but for the Nativity (June 24th). The banquet is over, the table has been cleared, and Salome enters bearing her promised reward on a platter. With a deep curtsey she holds it out before Herod. In earlier representations the princess is sometimes an acrobat, and here she bends back so far that without the strong vertical of her white veil she would seem in danger of falling. Herod and an elegant young man look down at the head whereas the other courtiers watch intently for the Queen's reaction. Herodias, who plotted the death, leans away and calmly, without looking down, she plunges a knife in the temple. Herod, beneath his scarlet canopy, half rises and raises a hand in horror.

The *Golden Legend* does not describe this act of Herodias, which is in general little known and perhaps represented here for the first time. Jerome records it, but Jean de Berry and his entourage had almost certainly seen visual evidence. During the Fourth Crusade the supposed head of St. John was brought from Constantinople and placed in a chapel in the cathedral of Amiens. Set in a reliquary in the form of a platter such as Salome carries here, the skull was only partially enclosed, and pilgrims were told that a cleft in the left temple had been made by Herodias' knife.[12] The chapel of the Baptist had been recently rebuilt by Cardinal Jean La Grange, who was prominent at the court of Charles V, the brother of Jean de Berry. Among the statues placed around the chapel was that of the King. Jean de Berry often visited Amiens; in fact, in the winter of 1407—when the painting of the *Belles Heures* was far advanced—he spent a week there. With his devotion to the Baptist and his passion for relics it seems probable that the Duke himself, or one of his clerics, suggested a miniature that would show Herodias enacting her vengeful deed.

Fol. 215   Death of Simon Magus. *Mass of Sts. Peter and Paul.*

The first of two miniatures celebrating the apostles most closely connected with the establishment of the Church in Rome bears the Duke's arms *(France ancien)*. It tells the apocryphal story of their challenge to Simon the Magus, who is mentioned briefly in Acts 8 : 9–24.

The Emperor and his court have gathered on the hill of the Capitol to watch the magician ascend, as he said he would, to heaven. The kneeling apostles face the tower, Peter, distinguished by his key, in buff and Paul in a rose mantle. At Peter's command the devils bearing Simon become visible and flee so that the magician, small but unmistakable because of his pointed hat, falls to his death. Although the colors are Paul's he did not paint this miniature. The figures, especially Nero, with his stock gesture of dismay, awkward stance, flattened nose, and hat with curling brim, are more reminiscent of Herman.

Simon's fall is not frequently represented and we have found no precedent either for the composition or the setting. A flight of steps leads to an inner doorway, and again in the Limbourgs' *Plan of Rome* in the *Très Riches Heures* the Capitol is approached by steps, though there they are exterior ones. The walls supporting the elaborate parapet of the Capitol consist of broken masonry filled with red brick, suggesting a restored ancient ruin.

Fol. 215v   Martyrdom of Sts. Peter and Paul.

Mass of Sts. Peter and Paul.

Angered at the death of Simon, Nero condemned the two apostles. Paul's decapitated corpse still remains crouched, blood spurting from the neck. According to Roman tradition his head struck the ground twice before coming to rest, and springs burst forth giving the site its name of Tre Fontane. Although the *Golden Legend* does not describe this miracle two small pools on the greensward are proof that it was known to the painter.

An elderly man whispers in Nero's ear and holds aloft a scarlet hood. Although seldom represented this can only be the hood Plautilla gave to Paul on his way to execution; she was cured of her blindness when she received it back soaked in his blood. In the miniature, however, a more urgent matter claims the Emperor's attention than Plautilla's hood. Peter, dressed in yellow-buff as in the previous miniature, kneels ready for decapitation and the executioner raises his sword, already stained with Paul's blood. Peter's presence is unexpected because, although both aspostles died on the same day, he was crucified upside down. According to the *Golden Legend* death by the sword was reserved for citizens of Rome. Can it be that Nero is being reminded that only Paul could claim the privilege?

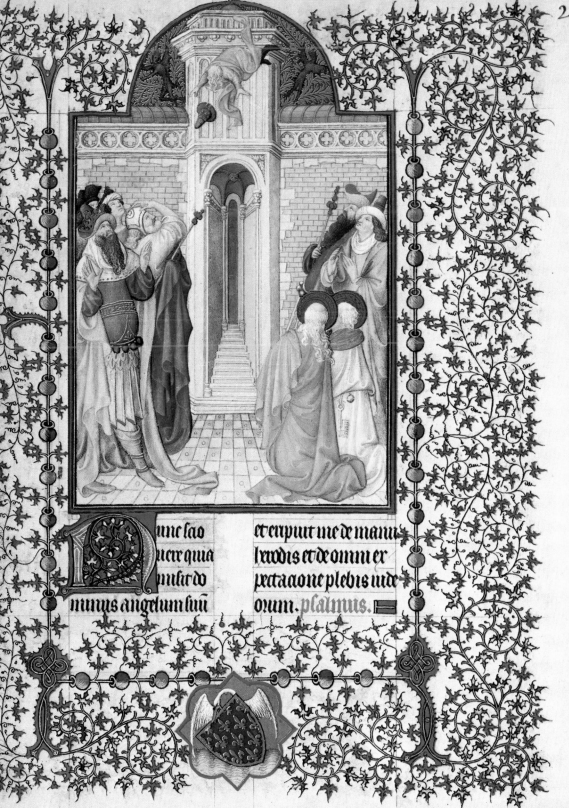

nunc sao
quer quia
mittar do
minus angelum suū

et eripuit me de manu
herodis et de omni ex
pectaaone plebis iude
orum. psalmus.

Et petrus ad se reu ers dixit. Nunc sao. Gloria patri et filio. Nunc sao neir

Kyrieleison. xpe Deus qui oõo. hodiernam diem apostolorum

Gaudeamus
omnes in
domino di
em festum celebrantes

sub honore sanctorum
omnium de quorum
sollempnitate gaudent
angeli et collaudant fi

Probably no earlier painting had gone as far as this in expressing by light the splendor of the celestial realm. Alongside the highly burnished gold disks and rays Paul has given the Madonna a bright yellow radiance, and all the colors are held at a high value. The two largest seraphim and a few saints have even assimilated the golden light of the principal figures.

The Madonna, like the one on 209, belongs to Paul's new type of celestial image. She and her child are monumental, yet Paul has adroitly eliminated the lower part of her body. The swirls of her mantle mask it, allowing the impression that it disappears in the light or behind the frame of the aureole. At her sides are St. Paul and St. Peter. Above stand the Baptist, name saint of the Duke, and John the Evangelist, whose vision of the multitude adoring the Lamb is the lesson of the Mass. Instead of the Lamb or the Trinity usual in representations of All Saints Paul has chosen the Madonna combined with a Trinity. Striving to show the vastness of the host the painter has abandoned medieval principles by obliterating the faces of many saints, leaving only a rim of hair or of the halo. Paul has here applied the perspective and drastic over-lapping that he learned from Trecento painting. The composition discloses, too, his deep understanding of Florentine geometry. Along the central axis there are three principal circles, each doubled or tripled. They are echoed by the rings of saints and, on a smaller scale, by the wheel of Catherine and Margaret's dragon, bent into a corre-sponding arc.

Fol. 221   Mass for All Souls.   PAUL

Monks praying around a bier was the usual illustration for the Office of the Dead (99), but since the Limbourgs had created a novel composition for that Office they could use the praying monks for a Mass that is uncommon in a Book of Hours. The requiem for All Souls is celebrated before an empty coffin covered by a simple black pall marked with a cross. Perhaps because Paul wanted to delineate clearly a chapel in a cemetery, which opens directly onto the greensward, he retained the traditional com-bination of an exterior and interior view. Once again he showed only a comparatively small section of a large building which extends vividly beyond the frames. Because this is not a narrative but a liturgical miniature he focused attention on the catafalque of the universal dead. We can see the features of only one of the hooded monks; of his fellows even less is visible, a back or impersonal hands, folded or turning the pages of books. Pale greens and browns, deepening to the rich black of the pall, predominate within, set off by the gold candlestick, flickering red flames, and the white parchment of books. Light enters the somber chapel through the arch and the high silver windows. A strip of cloudless blue sky contrasts with the melancholy interior.

Equiem etern̄ā | m ſyon et tibi reddetur
dona eis dn̄e et | notum in iherusalem.
lux perpetua luceat eis. pſ. | Exaudi oronem meā
Te decet hympnus deus | ad te omnis caro ueiet.

Ad incipiendam viam suam in exitu domus, ville vel loci.

In viam pacis salutis et prosperitatis dirigat dominus ihesus christus

Fol. 223v   The Duke on a Journey. *Prayer for Travelers.*

PAUL AND JEAN

This miniature illustrates a prayer for a safe journey which is either extremely rare or unprecedented in earlier Books of Hours. The Duke introduced it into three of his manuscripts. Here, in the earliest instance, the miniature is painted on a single leaf in a small gathering at the end of the manuscript, and since the borders differ somewhat from preceding ones the gathering was probably added at the end of the work. The Duke may well have become interested in this prayer, we suggest, because of an event in 1407 that shook him deeply, the murder of one of his nephews, Duke Louis d'Orléans, by another, Jean sans Peur, Duke of Burgundy. After this the struggle between the Burgundian party and their opponents, the Armagnacs, became extremely bitter, and no one in France could feel safe, least of all a leading Armagnac such as Jean de Berry. Some relationship to these grim events the miniature in the *Belles Heures* certainly has, because the banners on the chateau to which the Duke is riding bear the blue and gold bands of Burgundy. The peace of the realm depended upon the relationship between the two political parties, and Jean de Berry was a principal mediator. He may therefore be represented here on a symbolic or even an actual journey. Hoping in fact in January 1408 to negotiate an arrangement with Jean sans Peur that would prevent a major civil war, Jean de Berry went to meet him at Ypres.

Paul has given the chateau a powerful volume that foreshadows his famous portrayal of the Louvre in the *Très Riches Heures.* He placed the building in the foreground and he clearly wanted to show it from top to bottom, perhaps because it represents a specific Burgundian possession. As a result it is proportionately small for the figures and not directly accessible.

To give the impression of movement and a sudden arrival Paul has boldly shown the figures emerging from the space behind the right frame, and even the Duke is not yet entirely visible. The foremost riders are just reining up, and the horses twist to one side or another as they do at that moment, swaying in a beautiful rhythmical pattern. The white horse of Jean de Berry is a sign of his eminence. Three of the Duke's companions turn to look at him inquiringly as he sits quietly, apparently thoughtful just before the arrival at the gate. He looks older than in the portrait earlier in the book, and now wears a brown moustache and beard. All the figures lack luminosity and there are scarcely any spatial intervals between them, so that they seem to have been painted by Jean.

Notes to Introduction

1. *Prayerbook of Bonne of Luxembourg.*
2. Paris, Bibl. nat., fr. 166.
3. In addition to the two by the Limbourgs these Books of Hours are: *Très Belles Heures de Notre-Dame, Petites Heures, Brussels Hours,* and *Grandes Heures.* For all these see Meiss, Bibliography, 1967.
4. The prayer and miniature for a traveler (223v) had not appeared in earlier prayerbooks of the Duke, and rarely if ever in an earlier manuscript.
5. The text below the last miniature of the Heraclius cycle is the Suffrage (157), and below the last miniature of the Baptist cycle is the Introit of the Mass (212v).
6. See the early publication of the text from a manuscript, *Vie de nostre benoit sauveur Jesus Christ,* Lyons, Guillaume Leroy, before 1480.
7. Paris, Bibl. nat., fr. 242, about 1402.
8. Meiss, *Painting in Florence and Siena after the Black Death,* Princeton, 1951 (or New York, 1973), pp. 107–109.
9. "Secuntur misse. Et primo de nativitate domini n[ost]ri ih[es]u xr[ist]i. Et primo ponitur vita beati ieronimi tota ystoriata." The odd repetition of "Et primo" suggests that the rubric is itself composite, reflecting two stages of thought.
10. Oxford, Bodleian Lib., Douce 144.
11. Leonardo da Vinci, *Treatise on Painting,* trans. A. P. McMahon, Princeton, 1956, I, p. 85. For a similar thought see *The Notebooks of Leonardo da Vinci,* ed. E. MacCurdy, New York, 1938, II, p. 296.

Notes to Commentaries

1. See J. Plummer in the Bibliography.

2. Brussels, Bibl. royale, ms. 10376–77, fol. 16v. Tournai, 1352 (see Bibliography, Meiss, 1974, fig. 465).
3. Paris, Archives nat., J 187B no. 41.
4. See Meiss, 1974, fig. 319.
5. The suicide of Judas appears in the Way to Calvary for the first time in this miniature and in the nearly contemporary one in the Louvre that probably belonged to the *Grandes Heures*—another instance of a relationship between the Duke's two books.
6. The Nailing was first represented in France, soon after the *Vie* was written, in the Duke's *Très Belles Heures de Notre-Dame.*
7. Christ's Crown of Thorns here, as in the *Entombment* (152) and the *Descent* (80), consists of rushes bound together at intervals, like the relic then in the Sainte-Chapelle and now in Notre-Dame.
8. *Lorenzo Ghibertis Denkwürdigkeiten,* ed. J. von Schlosser, Berlin, 1972, p. 41.
9. See Meiss, 1974, fig. 716.
10. For Augustine on Virgil as a prophet see his *Sermo contra Judaeos, Paganos et Arianos* (Migne, *Pat. Lat.* XLII, col. 1125 ff.). Liturgical Nativity plays at Limoges and Rheims greeted the appearance of Virgil with "Vates Maro gentilium, da Christo testimonium."
11. The single upraised finger might also illustrate Virgil's recognition that, with the appearance of the Lamb, "the great line of the centuries begins anew" *(Fourth Eclogue).*
12. For the history of the relic and a gold reliquary plate probably given by Queen Isabeau in 1385 see M. Dusevel, *Histoire de la ville d'Amiens,* Amiens, 1832, II, p. 454 ff.; J. Corblet, *Hagiographie du diocèse d'Amiens,* Paris, IV, 1874, p. 336 ff.

Commentaries on Black and White Illustrations

Folio 24. **St. Mark** sits writing in a high, vaulted chamber. His symbol, the winged lion, occupies an exterior lean-to. Unlike the haloes of other Evangelists (22, 23) Mark's is of gold rays.

Folio 66v. **David makes a Thank-offering** *(Psalm 32)*. Holding a splendid gold reliquary, he kneels before an open shrine or chapel. The Lord's gesture illustrates his promise: "I will instruct thee and teach thee in the way which thou shalt go." Paul may have designed the robust figure of David but Herman probably painted the miniature.

Folio 67v. **David transfixed by Arrows** *(Psalm 38)*. He has fallen back on a deep, tiled floor, which resembles Jerome's on 183v. He calls for mercy from the wrathful Lord: "For thy arrows stick fast in me . . ." The Psalm is sung on Good Friday and the Lord's gesture illustrates the verse "But I, as a deaf man, heard not; and I was as a dumb man that openeth not his mouth."

Folio 68v. **David rebuked by the Prophet Nathan** *(Psalm 51)*. This is the usual illustration for the Psalm. Nathan gestures to heaven and points an accusing finger at the King, because he has taken Bathsheba and sent her husband to his death. David, wrapped like Nathan in a voluminous cloak, shrinks back toward the portcullised gate.

Folio 70. **David calls on the Lord** *(Psalm 102)* from the caves where, as a young man, he took refuge from the anger of King Saul. The dramatic figure of the youthful David, with head thrown back and foreshortened face, is a fourteenth-century French *topos* that was developed by Paul in the Catherine and Litany cycles. Red and gold rays emanate from the Lord, who ". . . hath looked down from the height of his sanctuary . . . to loose those that are appointed to death."

Folio 72. **David flees from Absalom** *(Psalm 143)*, in accordance with the Vulgate title for this Psalm. The King raises his hands beseechingly as he gallops round a bend, closely followed by his rebellious son. As in Paul's *Flight* (63) the horses leave hoofprints on the road. In its compact, forceful design the miniature resembles the first in the series (66) and it is no doubt by the same painter—Herman.

Folio 88. **The Assumption of the Virgin** illustrates her Fifteen Joys. Cherubim transport the tall, slender Mary to a strikingly foreshortened Deity, who raises his hand in blessing. A church marked the site of the Assumption in Jerusalem, and in an adjoining chapel David was said to have composed the Psalms. Perhaps the King in the lower miniature praying with his followers represents the author of the Psalter.

f. 24

f. 66v

f. 67v

f. 68v

f. 70

f. 72

nous pue que nous
mueillies puer uñe cher
fils quil mueille auoir
merci de moy et que il
me donnt en telle man
iere uiure que ie puisse
uenir a sa misencorde.
et en la fin uraye con
fession et repentance de
tous les pechez que ie
fis onques et me doit

Soulec dame
de misencoz
de mere de
dieu fontaine de tous
biens qui portastes ihe
sucrist. ix. mops en uos
precieux flans et laita
stes de nos doulces ma
melles. Belle uesdouce
dame ie uo pue mercy et

f. 158   f. 160v   f. 162v

f. 159   f. 160   f. 163

Folio 158. **St. Michael** overcoming the devil has already defeated his adversary in single combat. The youthful, fully armed archangel tramples his fallen opponent, who tenses his muscles in a last effort to tear apart the chain that holds him. Although the devil's wings and extremities are beastlike, his body and expressive face are intensely human—unlike his fellows on 141v and 170.

Folio 159. **St. John the Evangelist** is, as usual, young and beardless. The author of a Gospel, two Epistles and the Apocalypse, he holds a scroll and a goblet from which emerges a snake, symbolizing the powers of evil. The *Golden Legend* tells that the High-priest of Ephesus challenged him to drink from a poisoned cup; he drank and was unharmed.

Folio 160. **St. Andrew** is distinguished by the diagonal cross on which he was said to have suffered martyrdom. He holds it not quite upright but inclined to the left, with one bar resting on a fold of his tunic. His head and his glance are turned in the opposite direction. Jean de Berry was born on St. Andrew's Day but the *Belles Heures*, unlike some of the Duke's other books, does not give the saint special prominence.

Folio 160v. **St. James the Greater,** looking extremely lifelife, stands on the altar of a tall shrine. Two suppliants kneel before him, equipped like the saint with pilgrim's hat, scrip, and staff. It was the custom in Paris for a member of the pilgrim confraternity of Saint-Jacques-de-la-Boucherie to impersonate the saint in a procession on his feast day. The painter, Jean, might also have seen a large seated statue of St. James on the altar of that church.

Folio 162v. **St. Lawrence** on the gridiron is a very ambitious composition for so small a format. Jean, who painted this miniature, has piled the wood under the grill so that the saint is tipped forward and suffers martyrdom in full view. Lawrence and the youth working the bellows are rather close to figures in miniatures in the same gathering where Jean, or Herman, collaborated with Paul. The saint himself resembles Bartholomew on 161, and the youth blowing the fire could derive from the young man gathering stones on 162.

Folio 163. **St. Vincent** cast out to the beasts lies in a wilderness among barren peaks. Two lions and a wolf have gathered to devour the corpse but a disproportionately large crow swoops down to attack the wolf and, according to the Breviary, to defend the martyr's remains. Vincent was a popular saint in Paris, where the church of Saint-Germain-des-Prés was built to house his relics.

Folio 163v. **St. Clement cast into the Sea.** A little group of sailors dumps overboard the exiled pontiff, weighted by an anchor and wearing his triple tiara. Wind fills the sail and waves break around the bow of the ship, which is identical to the craft in other scenes in the book (168, 173, 185, 191v, 193).

Folio 165v. **St. Sebastian transfixed by Arrows.** The design suggests a model on a greater scale adapted to the dimensions of a miniature. In an effort to maintain large figures and to include both the archers and the saint the painter, Jean, has arrived at a crowded composition.

Folio 166v. **The Decapitation of St. Denis and his Companions.** Jean's miniature is impressive for the careful differentiation of the figures of the martyrs and for the agile headsman furiously swinging his axe to decapitate his last victim. The first to suffer death has fallen forward with blood spurting from his neck. St. Denis, Bishop of Paris, is headless but he remains kneeling, his mitered head in his hands. He was said to have walked with it from Montmartre to the site of the royal Abbey of Saint-Denis.

Folio 172. **St. Ambrose** baptizing three blond, curly-haired children in a wooden tub seems to be unique in the iconography of the fourth-century Bishop of Milan. He wrote a treatise on baptism and he is famous for having baptized the adult St. Augustine (41, p. 265), but the miniature seems to allude to some specific occasion. Possibly the rubric in red referring to Ambrose was written after the painting. Gregory is commemorated on the same folio and, unlike Ambrose, he is named in a prayer. If the painter (Jean or Herman?) thought he was illustrating Gregory the Great the miniature could show him baptizing the three blond Anglo-Saxon youths who impressed him so deeply in the slave market of Rome.

Folio 172v. **St. Augustine,** seated on the ground and inscribing a scroll like the Evangelist Matthew on 22, is evidently at work on his treatise on the Trinity. He looks up to contemplate a vision of God the Father holding the crucified Christ, but, strangely, the Holy Ghost in the form of a dove who normally floats between them is missing.

Folio 175v. **St. Bernard** as first abbot of Clairvaux holds a crozier, and in his other hand an impressively thick book, perhaps a reference to his many theological writings. Jean has painted the saint as a pensive young man clothed in black, although the Cistercians, to distinguish themselves from the unreformed Benedictines, normally wear white. However, he draws up his habit on one side to expose a white tunic beneath.

f. 163v

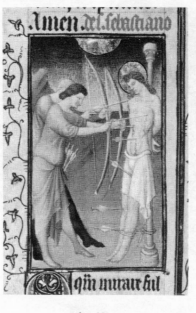

f. 165v

f. 166v

f. 172

f. 172v

f. 175v

f. 176v

f. 178

f. 179

f. 180

f. 181

Folio 176v. **St. Mary Magdalen,** kneeling to wipe Christ's foot with her hair, resembles Paul's St. Catherine before the executioner (19v). Here, however, Jean has covered almost all her face with her long tresses. Christ, looking down at her, raises a hand in blessing. The scene is set in a green landscape before a blue sky, whereas according to the Gospels Christ was reclining at a dinner. The composition recalls another encounter of the Magdalen with Christ—the Noli Me Tangere, when she mistakes the risen Savior for a gardener.

Folio 178. **St. Agnes,** who dedicated herself to Christ and rejected a powerful Roman suitor, is led to a brothel. A fleece of golden hair miraculously covers her naked body. The representation is rare. It was not included among the scenes of the saint on the royal cup given by the Duke of Berry to King Charles VI, now in the British Museum. Perhaps the painter had seen an Italian image of the Magdalen clad only in her hair (fresco, S. Domenico, Pistoia).

Folio 179. **St. Agatha,** like Catherine in 17, is tied to a column. As in that miniature one of the torturers presses his raised knee against the saint's rounded belly. Here he stretches to work the outsize pincers with which he and his comrade are removing her breasts. As usual Jean, the painter, has transformed Paul's strong and steadfast Catherine into a graceful and more pathetic martyr.

Folio 180. **St. Cecilia beheaded in the Bath.** The Limbourgs usually reserved a background of fleurs-de-lys for royalty (174) or for the patron saints of members of the royal family (158v). Perhaps it denotes here the emperor's own bath, where this early Christian martyr was at first boiled and then beheaded. Jean, who painted the miniature, might have seen in a window of Bourges cathedral the executioner grasping the saint by her hair as he raises his sword to decapitate her. There the artist told the story by depicting a fire beneath the cauldron whereas here the illuminator described the seething surface of boiling water.

Folio 181. **St. Geneviève,** with her slender torso and swirling mantle spreading in elegant folds around her feet, could only have been painted by Jean. The text compares her to the Wise Virgins who filled their lamps with oil, and she seems completely unaware of the imp above who is trying to extinguish her candle. An angel, however, holds a burning taper with which he defends the flame. Although the center of the Duke's domain was Bourges, he resided in Paris and his arms in the border associate him with the patron saint of that city.

Folio 199v. **The Ascension.** Jean chose an established iconographical type that shows Christ rising into a cloud. The imprints of the feet on the mountain are often represented. The Virgin is a remarkably youthful figure in white, her long, fair hair partly covered by a voluminous blue cloak. Only one of the fourteen disciples who accompany her can be securely identified—St. Peter, with his short square beard, pointing upwards.

Folio 205v. **The Elevation of the Host** illustrates the Mass for Corpus Christi. The altar is set beneath an architectural canopy and the priest—a monk—raises the wafer. Behind the server, who holds a large candle, three worshipers kneel in adoration on the greensward while a tonsured figure throws up his hands in wonder. The painter, Herman, did not finish the base of a chalice or monstrance on the altar, and at the center he drew Christ on the cross and, to the right, a figure—probably St. John—but he left them unpainted.

Folio 207v. **The Exaltation of the Cross.** The painter, Herman, shows a man and a woman kneeling before a large arcaded altar on which, between two candles, stands a cross hung with the Crown of Thorns and with the birch and scourge used in the Flagellation (132). The portly man is apparently neither a king nor emperor, and thus not Constantine or Heraclius, who are both associated with the story of the cross. His companion in her ample draperies is equally enigmatic.

Folio 41. **Sts. Ambrose and Augustine.** They hold the text of the *Te deum*. This canticle of praise, in Matins of the Hours of the Virgin, is said to have been composed by them on the occasion of Augustine's baptism. Golden rays descend from, or rather through, the keystone of the vault on the divinely inspired hymn.

Folio 93. **Adoration of the Cross.** Two worshipers kneel at an altar, looking up at a simple wood cross on a stepped base from which the Crown of Thorns is suspended. The painter has exploited the tall narrow format to depict the full height of a vaulted church. Although the two nearest windows of the clerestory are traceried he did not yet attempt to simulate glazing or luminosity. In later miniatures windows are leaded (96, 97v), and finally they become translucent (184v, 194v, 221). Here the uniform pale green of windows and walls permits an uninterrupted sweep to the vaults that enhances the impression of height.

f. 199v

f. 205v

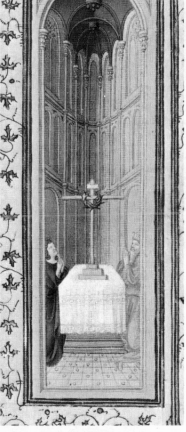

f. 93

f. 207v

f. 41

Observations on the Make-up and Decoration of the Manuscript

BY JOHN PLUMMER

The gatherings of the *Belles Heures,* with the numbers of their leaves superscribed and with the numbers of their inclusive folios in parentheses, may be described as follows: 1^2(A–1), 2^{12}(2–13), 3^7(14–20), 4^9(21–29), 5^8(30–37), 6^8(38–45), 7^8(46–53), 8^8(54–61), 9^8(62–69), 10^{10}(70–79), 11^8(80–87), 12^6(88–93), 13^5(94–98), 14^8(99–106), 15^8(107–114), 16^8(115–122), 17^8(123–130), 18^8(131–138), 19^8(139–146), 20^8(147–154), 21^8(155–162), 22^8(163–170), 23^8(171–178), 24^4(179–182), 25^7(183–190),* 26^5(191–194), 27^8(195–202), 28^8(203–210), 29^8(211–218), 30^4(219–222), 31^3(223–225). If one disregards the pictorial gatherings (3, 13, 25, and 26), which consist of either four or six leaves of miniatures plus one blank leaf, it becomes clear that the remaining textual gatherings were originally written in gatherings of eight leaves, except 2 which has twelve leaves for the calendar; 4 which originally had eight, but has lost one leaf and gained two blanks; 10 which has two added leaves that were inserted into the original eight (the insertion guide marks can be seen on fols. 74v and 75); 12 with six leaves is textually complete in itself and seems an addition to the original plan; 24 and 30, each with a half gathering of four leaves, which complete the texts of the Suffrages and the Masses; and 31 whose three leaves, with a blank unruled page at the beginning and end, appear to be an afterthought. It is also clear that the original scribal plan based on gatherings of eight has been altered and enlarged in a number of ways. In which ways and in what order are summarily discussed below.

The combined evidence of the unused pages at the ends of gatherings 10 and 16, of the half-length gatherings 24 and 30, and of the original scribal catchwords written in a *bâtarde* script show that the manuscript was written in the following units: gatherings 5–10, 14–16, 17–20, 21–24, 27–28, 29–30. A second kind of catchword, written in a Gothic minuscule probably by the original editor, has been erased and trimmed in binding, but two examples can still be read under ultraviolet light. On folio 87v one can make out the word "placebo," the antiphon that begins the Office of the Dead. It proves that gathering 11 (Hours of the Cross and of the Holy Spirit) was to have been followed by gathering 14 (Office of the Dead) and that gatherings 12 (Fifteen Joys) and 13 (Diocrès-Bruno cycle) are intrusions. A second example occurs at the end of gathering 20 (fol. 154v) and reads "d̄ne labia." It shows that gathering 20 (Office of the Passion) was originally followed by gathering 11 with the Hours of the Cross and of the Holy Spirit or by some other Office or Hours that is now missing. The evidence for these alternatives is inconclusive. A third kind of catchword, possibly added by the binder, occurs on folios 122v and 210v, but they reflect the present order and tell us nothing new.

To the earliest rubrics written in minium were added others written in a purplish red ink that was also used in the legends of the pictorial cycles. They probably were added as part of a second and expanded plan for the manuscript. This is the only reddish ink found in gatherings 4 and 12: the former may not have been part of the original plan; the latter almost certainly was not. The same ink was used at the end of gathering 20 (fol. 154v), where mention is made of the Suffrages that now follow, but we know from the erased catchword on the same page that some Office or Hours had originally been planned for this place. This ink was also used on folio 182v for the rubrics of the Masses and the Jerome cycle and is thereby connected to the stage at which the pictorial cycles were added.

A study of the decoration shows clearly that the book was in general decorated from front to back, and also that some gatherings were not decorated in their present order. Such gatherings are 2 (calendar) which was apparently done last, 3 (Catherine cycle) whose motifs belong with gatherings 21–30, 4 (Gospel selections) which has some motifs that only occur again in gathering 14, and 11 (Hours of the Cross and of the Holy Spirit) whose decoration belongs to the later stage of gatherings 21–30. Folios 73–74v (Gregory cycle) were not decorated with the rest of gathering 10, but were instead done at about the same stage as the Catherine cycle and gatherings 21–30. All of the other gatherings, with the unexplained exception of 7, appear to have been decorated in their present sequence.

The *Belles Heures* was originally conceived as a rather modest manuscript. Before the writing of the Office of the Passion, that is, before gathering 17, the plan included only single miniatures at the beginnings of various texts and omitted gatherings 3 (Catherine cycle), 4 (Gospel selections), 12 (Fifteen Joys), and 13 (Diocrès-Bruno cycle) and folios 73–74v (Gregory cycle). With the Office of the Passion, the scribe left space for multiple miniatures, and with the Suffrages, for picture cycles with their own special legends. This revised and augmented plan also included the insertion of the extra gatherings in the earlier part of the book. The new plan reveals the desire of the Limbourgs, in concert with the Duke of Berry, to continually enlarge their ambitions and to surpass their own achievements.

*Through a mistake in foliation, there is no folio 188.

Provenance and Binding of the *Belles Heures*

In 1417, a year after the death of the Duke of Berry, the *Belles Heures* was purchased by Yolande, Duchess of Anjou. During the following two decades, and occasionally even later, its miniatures and/or drawings of them served as models for illuminators, many of them in western and northwestern France. Notable among these copies are miniatures in the *Rohan Hours*, in the Spitz Hours, and by the Rohan Master as well as the Master of Marguerite d'Orléans (see Meiss, *The Limbourgs*, 1974, pp. 256–277). After that time we lose trace of the manuscript until 1880, when it was sold by the d'Ailly family to Baron Edmond de Rothschild. The manuscript passed to Baron Maurice de Rothschild, from whom the Cloisters acquired it in 1954.

At that time the manuscript bore a green morocco binding of the seventeenth century. This binding was excessively tight, and the necessity to unbind the book for the photography for this facsimile provided an opportunity to rebind properly. This work was done in 1972 by Miss Deborah Evetts, binder of the Pierpont Morgan Library. The sewing holes of the original binding of 1408–1409 were reused, as they had been also in the seventeenth century.

Bibliographical References

THE MANUSCRIPT

Millard Meiss, with the assistance of S. O. Dunlap Smith and E. H. Beatson, *French Painting in the Time of Jean de Berry, The Limbourgs and their Contemporaries*, New York and London, 1974. This book includes the first comprehensive study of the *Belles Heures* and of the Limbourgs, and a full bibliography.

Jean Porcher, *Les Belles Heures de Jean de France, duc de Berry*, Paris, 1953.

New York, Metropolitan Museum, The Cloisters, *The Belles Heures of Jean, Duke of Berry Prince of France*, ed. J. J. Rorimer and M. B. Freeman, New York, 1958.

John Plummer, "A Blank Page in the *Belles Heures*," in *Gatherings in Honor of Dorothy E. Miner* (in press).

THE DUKE OF BERRY

Françoise Lehoux, *Jean de France, duc de Berri. Sa vie. Son action politique. 1340–1416*, Paris, 1966–1968. 4v.

Millard Meiss, *French Painting in the Time of Jean de Berry. The Late XIV Century and the Patronage of the Duke*, London and New York, 1967. 2v. 2nd ed. 1969.

SOME RELIGIOUS SOURCES

The Golden Legend of Jacobus de Voragine, tr. and adapted by G. Ryan and H. Ripperger, New York, 1941. (In the preparation of this facsimile, however, we have used the text of the French translation as it appears in the manuscript Paris, Bibl. nat., fr. 242, of ca. 1402.)

Meditations on the Life of Christ, ed. I. Ragusa and R. B. Green, Princeton, 1961.

Vie de nostre benoit sauveur Jesus Christ, Lyon, Guillaume Leroy before 1480.

Ogier d'Anglure, *Le saint voyage de Jherusalem*, ed. F. Bonnardot and A. Longnon (Société des anciens textes français, X), Paris, 1878.

Other Manuscripts by the Limbourgs

Chantilly, Musée Condé, *Très Riches Heures*.

Paris, Bibliothèque nationale, *Bible moralisée*.

Vatican Library, Valerius Maximus. (For information about all these, and the following manuscripts, see the Bibliography, item 1, p. 268.)

Single Miniatures by the Limbourgs inserted in Manuscripts:

Paris, Bibliothèque nationale, *Petites Heures de Jean de Berry*, fol. 228v. *Très Belles Heures de Notre-Dame*, pp. 225, 240.

Closely Related Manuscripts

London, British Museum, *Breviary of Jean sans Peur*.

London, Count Antoine Seilern, Book of Hours.